WATCHMAN ON THE WALL

Man Your Post

TRAINING MANUAL

Deirdre Burnette

authorHOUSE°

AuthorHouse™
1663 Liberty Drive
Bloomington, IN 47403
www.authorhouse.com
Phone: 833-262-8899

Published by AuthorHouse 01/31/2023

ISBN: 978-1-7283-7891-6 (sc)
ISBN: 978-1-7283-7892-3 (e)

Library of Congress Control Number: 2023931756

Print information available on the last page.

Any people depicted in stock imagery provided by Getty Images are models, and such images are being used for illustrative purposes only. Certain stock imagery © Getty Images.

This book is printed on acid-free paper.

Because of the dynamic nature of the Internet, any web addresses or links contained in this book may have changed since publication and may no longer be valid. The views expressed in this work are solely those of the author and do not necessarily reflect the views of the publisher, and the publisher hereby disclaims any responsibility for them.

TABLE OF CONTENTS

"But I will make you as unyielding and hardened as they are, I will make your forehead like the hardest stone, harder than flint. Do not be afraid of them or terrified by them, though they are a rebellious house."

(Ezekiel 3: 8-9) NIV

INTRODUCTION

In these apostate times that we are living in, the Lord's WATCHMAN/WATCHMEN are needed to take their position on the Wall.

Many WATCHMEN have fallen asleep or they are mingling with the social environment(s) thus being desensitized to the <u>true</u> spiritual climate.

The Lord's WATCHMAN 'must' acclimate to a sphere of sanctification (being set apart) and holiness (right standing) before our GOD... Jehovah Elohim.

The Lord's WATCHMAN 'see' a thing, long before it reaches the gaze of others. The Lord made His WATCHMAN/WATCHMEN that way. <u>Remaining acclimated to the sphere of sanctification and holiness is the Lord's WATCHMAN'S pulse.</u> The Lord's sphere is the force/Power that causes the Lord's WATCHMAN/WATCHMEN to live, move and have their being. When the Lord's WATCHMAN steps off the grid of sanctification and holiness, the 'imbalance' causes noticeable inertia. (Tendency not to move or act.)

The Lord's WATCHMAN 'must' remain in the Lord's timing and obedient surrender.

Date: _____

My NAME is...

_____

I am a WATCHMAN.

I remember when the LORD called me. Here is my story:

_____

_____

_____

_____

_____

_____

_____

_____

_____

_____

Amen.

PREVAILING CLIMATE/CONDITION
(of Jehovah's people)

Sin! Sin! Sin! UNCONFESSED SIN! The transgression against the law(s) of Jehovah Elohim has fostered a climate of repercussions, consequences, judgements, and Woe.

Many are refusing to *confess* their sins and wicked ways and have brought judgment upon themselves. Many are *unfaithful* to the message of repentance, converting and being transformed. Many have instead sought out alliances and co-workers who compromise with their sin, and heaped to themselves false Teachers/Leaders who lead them further and further astray because the Teachers/Leaders themselves are full of lusts and rebellions.

Many of Jehovah's people are watering down the GOSPEL... the GOOD NEWS. The WORD made flesh is the POWER to save, transform and sustain. However, many are not digesting/ studying the WORD, thus, are not rightly dividing the WORD. Many are not showing themselves approved workmen before our Father. Jehovah's people (those called by His NAME) have induced a state of darkness and rebellion before the Father. Continually sinning and constantly stiffening their necks; thus, not humbling themselves, praying, nor turning from their wicked ways. For only THEN... will the LORD hear from heaven, forgive sin, and heal the land.

Many of Jehovah's people have SINNED, and continue to walk in sin against the Lord Jehovah. Many of Jehovah's people have employed IDOL's; gods that are 'no gods' at all. Many of Jehovah's people have taken upon themselves cisterns, broken cisterns that can hold no water at all; instead, of calling upon the LORD, the SOURCE of 'living' water.

Many of Jehovah's people are professing the LORD with their lips, but their hearts are far from the LORD. Hoarding hearts of deceit and carnality, they are wicked imposters

NOTES...

who are set to ravage who they may, in the Body of Christ. You as a WATCHMAN will see these imposters as clear as day. WATCHMEN will detect and expose them that labor among the Body of Christ. That is what WATCHMEN do. We watch.

Watch: *Hedge about (as with thorns), that is, guard; protect, attend to, beware, keep(er), mark, look narrowly, observe, preserve, regard, reserve, save (self), wait (for), watch (man).*

(Reference: Strong's Definition)

WATCHMAN/WATCHMEN it is time to get back on THE WALL. (In your position.) You are a discerner of spirits. (Human spirits, Demonic spirits, or Holy Spirit.)

- You are a discerner whose perception(s) is sharpened and trained by the Courts of Heaven.
- You are a distinguisher between that which is Holy and that which is profane.
- You are a 'spiritual binocular', you view distant objects and discern whether it is friend or foe.
- You relay the information to those (gatekeepers) who have authority to allow passage or overturn entrance at the gate.
- You hold the duty in the spirit realm, of what the earth realm would equate to a 'Green Beret' soldier. You are a specially trained Soldier (in the Army of the LORD) who engages in Special Operations that ONLY YOU, the WATCHMAN, (as a trained Soldier in the Army of the LORD) can do.

You, the WATCHMAN have endured rigorous training (known and unknown), to induce the 'skill set' needed to carry out the mission/assignment(s) given to you. You are an AUTHORIZED SNIPER. Your critical OPERATION is from long range. You are an AUTHORIZED VESSEL unto the Lord. Protect your ARMOR. Guard your heart.

NOTES...

Skill Set: A person's range of skills or abilities.

(Reference: Oxford Languages)

Your skill set is YOUR knowledge and ability. Your skill set is your EXPERIENCE that will be needed to successfully fulfil your assignment.

It is crucial that you, THE WATCHMAN on the WALL... accept, embrace, learn, and protect your CALL. Your call is distinguished. NO MAN APPOINTS YOU. You are hand-picked of our FATHER. Taught and sustained by the person of THE HOLY GHOST and trained both in private and on the actual battlefield. You are 100% spiritually molded and made.

Always remember you are Special Op's (Operations), so you are on the LOW. Your assignment(s) are carried out through 'legal' engagement with the Spirit Realm. So, Intercession, Praise, and Worship are your MAJOR weapons. (We will touch on this in a later chapter.)

Many in the Body of Christ WILL NOT recognize you, nor understand your earth/life sojourn. Many will not understand your reason for being here. However, that comes with the position. You are 99% under cover, and more times than not, unidentified and misunderstood by most.

Them who you are sent to, will either accept your warning, or they will reject it. Gatekeepers, (those who hold Authority to execute STANDARD) will either reject or accept. However, their response is not in your (THE WATCHMAN's) control; BUT the blood will be OFF YOUR HAND.

Fellow WATCHMAN/WATCHMEN on the WALL, embrace your walk. Endure your training seasons. Cultivate your position on the Wall and understand who you are, and why you do what you do. Fellow WATCHMAN/WATCHMEN on the WALL, be fully persuaded in the CONFIDENCE afforded you... in Christ.

Be not afraid, but be of GOOD COURAGE... You are born, for such a time as this.

"In the LORD our God is the salvation of Israel."

NOTES...

See Below Referenced Scriptures.

• Jeremiah 3:25

A Watchman's prayer life and engagement with the spiritual realm is his/her arsenal.

• Death and life are in the power of your tongue, so remember that spiritual maturity is <u>mandatory</u>.

Much of your life has probably consisted of the rigors of trial and error and learning from your mistakes. Your lessons learned pushed, pulled, and propelled you into maturity.

"Return, faithless people," declares the LORD, "for I am your husband. I will choose you – one from a town and two from a clan – and bring you to Zion. Then I will give you shepherds after my own heart, who will lead you with knowledge and understanding."

(Jeremiah 3: 14-15) NIV

SECTION 1
The Lord's Purposes

THE LORD'S PURPOSES

NOTES: At A Quick Glance:	**EVERYTHING BEING DONE 'POINTS' TO THE KINGDOM OF GOD** • **Kingdom of God/Light** • **Kingdom of Heaven/Manifested on earth** • **Worship Him… or No?** • **Earthly Reign of Christ (Kingdom at hand)** • **Ambassador of Christ … or No?** *"For by him were all things created, that are in heaven, and in earth, visible and invisible, whether they be thrones, or dominions, or principalities, or powers: all things were created by him, and for him."* *(Colossians 1:16)* KJV
	Kingdom: Dominion, that is (abstractly) the estate (rule) Or (concretely) the country (realm): - kingdom, King's, reign, royal. (Reference: Strong's Concordance)
	The Kingdoms of this world belongs to the Lord and His Christ. Everything being done in the earth is bringing the high places low. Everything exalting itself above the knowledge of God will be cast down. The Kingdom of God and the Kingdom of Heaven, although similar… represents two different functions. **While the *Kingdom of God is the…** *Supreme Authority and Dominion of all Creation.* **The ** Kingdom of heaven is…** *The announcement of the Kingdom reign of Christ, the Messiah, manifested in the earth.*

*Kingdom of God/Light

"David praised the LORD in the presence of the whole assembly, saying, Praise be to you O LORD, God of our father Israel, from everlasting to everlasting.
Yours, O LORD, is the greatness and the power and the glory and the majesty and the splendor, for everything in heaven and earth is yours.
Yours O LORD, is the kingdom; you are exalted as head over all.
Wealth and honor comes from you; you are the ruler of all things.
In your hands are strength and power to exalt and give strength to all."

(1 Chronicles 29: 10-13) NIV

Everything belongs to GOD:

YAHWEH. (YHWH) Jehovah Elohim is eternal. His Kingdom will NEVER be destroyed. He is the Author and Finisher of our FAITH. The GREAT SHEPHERD. And the ONLY HOPE for our eternal life and security.

Holy and reverent is the LORD's name, HE has commanded His covenant forever. There is a system of redemption sent from the LORD, for His people. They that do his commandments have 'good' understanding.

Unto the upright there ariseth light in darkness.

Wisdom begins with 'fearing' the LORD. The scriptures teach that BLESSED is the man that fear the LORD.

Jehovah is our ETERNAL SHEPHERD:

If you are a citizen of God's Kingdom, you are secure. You are safe. You are an OVERCOMER.

You overcome because greater is He that is in you than he that is in the world. You overcome because whatsoever is born of God overcomes the world. We have victory through our FAITH.

Revelation twelve teaches that we must not love our lives unto the death. Remember, we overcome by the blood of the Lamb, and the word of our testimony.

The LORD'S Purposes

Counsel. Advice. Purpose. Plan.

See Below Referenced Scriptures.

- Psalm 111:9
- Psalm 112:4

> **"All the ends of the earth will remember and turn to the LORD, and all the families of the nations will bow down before him, for dominion belongs to the LORD and he rules over the nations."**
> **(Psalm 22:27-28) NIV**

"The Lord gives strength to all."

"The Lord is the greatness, power, glory, majesty and the splendor for EVERYTHING in heaven and earth."

The Lord's praise endures forever.

Israel Will Be Regathered:

"And the ransomed of the LORD shall return and come to Zion with songs and everlasting joy upon their heads: they shall obtain joy and gladness, and sorrow and sighing shall flee away."

(Isaiah 35:10) KJV

The book of Isaiah 35th chapter teaches us that there will be a highway and a way called "the way of holiness." We are taught that the unclean cannot pass over it.

We are taught that the eyes of the blind shall be opened, and the ears of the deaf shall be unstopped. The lame man will leap, and the tongue of the dumb will sing. The thirsty land will become springs of water.

Zion (the city of God) will be a joy. Everlasting joy.

The Lord is the King of glory and HE is strong and mighty in battle. The earth is the Lord's. And everything in it.

To you who are of a fearful heart... Be strong and fear not. Our Father will come with vengeance and he will save us.

He that has clean hands and a pure heart will ascend the hill of the Lord and stand in His holy place. We shall receive blessings and righteousness from the God of our salvation.

We are the generation of them that seek His face.

Keep your soul from vanity.

TEST YOUR KNOWLEDGE:

1. Wisdom Begins with fearing the Lord. True/False?

The LORD'S Purposes

Counsel. Advice. Purpose. Plan.

See Below Referenced Scriptures.

- Psalm 24:8
- Psalm 24:1
- Isaiah 35:4
- Psalm 24:3-6

Every Watchman's foundational motive is the restoration of Zion.

**Kingdom of Heaven

"In the time of those kings, the God of heaven will set up a kingdom that will never be *destroyed, nor will it be left to another people. It will crush all those kingdoms and bring them to an end, but it will itself endure forever.*"

(Daniel 2: 44-45) NIV

...it will crush:

(Psalm 2: 7-12) NIV

"He said to me, "You are my Son, today I have become your Father. Ask of me, and I will make the nations your inheritance, the ends of the earth your possession. You will rule them with an iron scepter, you will dash them to pieces like pottery.
Therefore, you kings, be wise; be warned, you rulers of the earth. Serve the Lord with fear and rejoice with trembling.
Kiss the Son, lest he be angry and you be destroyed in your way, for his wrath can flare up in a moment. Blessed are all who take refuge in him."

Son: Member of a group. People (of a nation) A member of a guild, order, class

Son: A son (as a builder of the family name) one born, branch, breed, very fruitful, worthy

(Reference: BDB/Strong's Definition)

In Psalm 2, the passage is speaking to David, the Israelite king; but also contrasting Christ the Eternal King.

The kingdoms of this world will become the kingdom of our Lord and His Christ. **Hallelujah! HE REIGNS!**

He <u>will</u> reign for ever and ever.

The LORD'S Purposes

Counsel. Advice. Purpose. Plan.

See Below Referenced Scriptures.

- Revelation 11:15

Worship Him… or No?

"Now therefore, if ye will obey my voice indeed, and keep my covenant, then ye shall be a peculiar treasure unto me above all people: for all the earth is mine: And ye shall be unto me a kingdom of priests, and a holy nation. These are the words which thou shalt speak unto the children of Israel."

(Exodus 19: 5-6) KJV

The Lord chose Israel not because Israel deserved it, but because of His love and mercy. The Lord chose Israel to represent His way of life. The Lord chose Israel to teach His Word, and to be an agent of the Lord's Salvation to the world. All nations of the world would be blessed through Abraham's descendants.

Idolatry

"And the children of Israel did evil in the sight of the Lord, and served Baalim and the groves."

Baalim: Supreme male divinity of the Phoenicians or Canaanites. The son of Jehiel and grandfather of Saul. A town of Simeon. The same as; Baal, a Phoenician deity.

"And they forsook the LORD and served Baal and Ashtaroth."

Baal: A Phoenician deity.
Ashtaroth: Ashtaroth or Astaroth = "star"

1. False goddesses in the Canaanite religion, usually related to fertility cult (female deity)
2. A city in Bashan east of the Jordan given to Manasseh

1. A Babylonian (Astarte)-Canaanite goddess (of fortune and happiness), the supposed consort of Baal, her images
   a. The goddess, goddesses
   b. Her images
   c. Sacred trees or poles set up near an altar

(Reference: BDB/Strong's Definition)

The LORD'S Purposes

Counsel. Advice. Purpose. Plan.

See Below Referenced Scriptures.

- Judges3:7

Groves: "groves (for idol worship)"

Deuteronomy eight and two teaches us that the Lord led the children of Israel in the wilderness for forty years to humble them, to prove them, and to know their hearts. Whether they would keep His commandments or not.

Physical Israel did then what spiritual Israel is now doing. Same idolatry, only repackaged.

Throughout Biblical and world history, the children of Israel (physical) did evil over and over again in the sight of the LORD and served Baalim and Ashtaroth and the gods of Syria.

There would be periods of evil. Then there would be periods of righteousness.

- Children of Israel cried unto the Lord.
- Then the children of Israel did put away Baalim and Ashtaroth, and served the LORD only.
- Took to wife Jezebel, the daughter of Ethbaal... and went and served Baal and worshipped him.
- "And he answered, I have not troubled Israel, but thou, and thy father's house, in that ye have forsaken the commandments of the LORD, and thou has followed Baalim."
- And he reared up an altar for Baal in the house of Baal which he had built in Samaria

The Prophet Elijah went to battle against the false prophets of Baal.

Elijah instructed that all Israel and the false prophets of Baal be gathered. He instructed that not one prophet of Baal escape.

Elijah asked... 'how long halt you between two opinions? If God be God follow Him... but if Baal... follow him.

The LORD God of Israel used the Prophet Elijah to do a mighty work. A work that, for Elijah, induced a witchcraft attack from Jezebel against him. A psychic attack that overwhelmed Elijah with fear and discouragement. (We will talk about this in a latter chapter.)

The LORD'S Purposes

Counsel. Advice. Purpose. Plan.

See Below Referenced Scriptures.

- Judges 10:6
- Judges 10:10
- 1 Samuel 7:4
- 1Kings 16:31
- 1 Kings 18:18
- 1 Kings 16:32

Earthly Reign of Christ (Kingdom at hand)

"In those days John the Baptist came, preaching in the Desert of Judea, and saying, "Repent, for the kingdom of heaven is near."

(Matthew 3:1-2) NIV

Kingdom: Royal power, kingship, dominion rule

    a. Not to be confused with an actual kingdom but rather the right or authority to rule over a kingdom
    b. Of the royal power of Jesus as the triumphant Messiah

(Reference: BDB/Strong's Definition)

Christ reigned to restore LIGHT by bringing redemption to a lost world. The PURPOSE being RESTORATION back to the Father.

"Blessed are the poor in spirit,
For theirs is the kingdom of heaven."
(Matthew 5:3) NIV

The LORD'S Purposes

Counsel. Advice. Purpose. Plan.

NOTES:

Ambassador of Christ... or No?

"A wicked messenger falleth into mischief: but a faithful ambassador is health."

(Proverbs 13:17) KJV

MESSENGER: Representative. From an unused root meaning to dispatch as a deputy; a messenger: specifically of God, that is, an angel (also a prophet, priest, or teacher): - ambassador, angel, king, messenger

AMBASSADOR: Messenger, pivot of door, hinge, (as pressed in turning) pang, distress, also a throe (as a physical or mental pressure); also a herald or errand doer (as constrained by the principal)

HEALTH: Health, healing, cure, profit, sound (of mind), a medicine, or (abstractly) a cure; deliverance, remedy, wholesome, yielding

(Reference: BDB/Strong's Definitions)

> Connection to the VINE and obedience to the Word of the Lord is your lifeline. To be an ambassador in good standing, you must stay the course. Lest you fall into mischief.

We are ambassadors sent on the Lord's behalf admonishing reconciliation unto God.

And we are to speak boldly. And we are to speak as we ought to speak.

The LORD'S Purposes

Counsel. Advice. Purpose. Plan.

See Below Referenced Scriptures.

- Jeremiah 49:14
- 2 Corinthians 5:20
- Ephesians 6:20

You are a Prophet/Watchman in the earth. A representative of the Kingdom of God.

Wicked:

guilty of sin, morally wrong

Mischief:

bad, unpleasant, evil, (giving pain, unhappiness, misery)

Faithful:

faithful, trusting, established, trustworthy

(Reference: BDB/Strong's Definition)

THE LORD'S PURPOSES: *Continued*

NOTES: At A Quick Glance:	**THERE IS A 'REMNANT' IN THE EARTH**
	 • **A 'Remnant' Preserved to the Lord** • **Have not bowed their knee to Baal** • **The 'whosoever' Will** *"Yet will I leave a remnant, that ye may have some that shall escape the sword among the nations, when ye shall be scattered through the countries."* *(Ezekiel 6:8)* KJV
	Remnant: To be left over, remain, preserve alive, have an excess. To cause to abound. Leave. ***Remnant:*** Survivor, remnant that which is left. (Reference: Strong's and BDB Definition)
	"Except the Lord of hosts had left unto us a very small remnant, we should have been as Sodom, and we should have been like unto Gomorrah." (Isaiah 1:9) KJV "In that day the remnant of Israel, the survivors of the house of Jacob, will no longer rely on him who struck them down but will truly rely on the Lord, the Holy One of Israel. A remnant will return, a remnant of Jacob will return to the Mighty God." (Isaiah 10:20-21) NIV

A REMNANT 'PRESERVED' TO THE LORD

"And I will make her that halted a remnant, and her that was cast far off a strong nation: and the LORD shall reign over them in mount Zion from henceforth, even for ever."

(Micah 4:7) KJV

"And God sent me before you to **preserve** you a **posterity** in the earth, and to **save your lives** by a **great deliverance**."

(Genesis 45:7) KJV

Even now there is a remnant according to the election of grace.

The Lord preserves a remnant. Even when it looks as if the works of darkness has overtaken and overwhelmed the earth, the Lord has a remnant. The plans of the Lord will not be overthrown.

Are you a remnant? Are you a survivor? Continue in "LIFE" my fellow Watchman.

- The remnant of Israel and they that have escaped of the house of Jacob, will in the appointed day rest upon the Lord, the Holy One of Israel in truth.

- The Lord delights in mercy. The Lord does not retain his anger forever. He is the Lord who pardons iniquity and passes by the transgression of His remnant.

"Esaias also crieth concerning Israel, though the number of the children of Israel be as the sand of the sea, a remnant shall be saved."

(Romans 9:27) KJV

The LORD'S Purposes

Counsel. Advice. Purpose. Plan.

See Below Referenced Scriptures.

- Romans 11:5
- Isaiah 10:20
- Micah 7:18

PRESERVE:
to put, set in place, lay, ordain, establish, appoint, constitute, determine, call (a name), consider

POSTERITY:
rest, residue, remainder, remnant, descendants,
residual (surviving, final) portion: that had escaped

SAVE YOUR LIVES:
to live, to have life, to continue in life, remain alive, to sustain life, nourish up, quicken, preserve, restore, revive

Great:
in intensity, in importance, distinguished, mighty, noble

DELIVERANCE:
escape, escaped remnant, an escaped portion

(Reference: BDB and Strong's Definition)

Even Our FAITH

Our faith saves us. We are to fear not, and believe only. This is where our peace is.

We are to bow our knees unto the Father of our Lord Jesus Christ and be strengthened with might by His Spirit in our inner man... that Christ may dwell in our hearts by faith. Rooted and grounded in love. This is the riches of His glory.

First and foremost we must 'cement the fact' that without faith it is **IMPOSSIBLE** to please God. The scriptures ask the question: "when the Lord comes, will he find faith in the earth?"

Through faith in the name of the Prince of Life, whom God has raised from the dead we are strong and have perfect soundness.

We must be established by faith, sanctified by faith, and be diligent to purify our hearts by faith. And equally importantly, be diligent that our faith fail us not.

We only have access to the Father, by FAITH. And our faith is counted for righteousness. There is NO OTHER WAY. We ABIDE BY FAITH. We must be diligent to walk by faith and stand fast in faith.

We must be diligent to examine ourselves and be certain that our faith is not vain. For we overcome the world by our FAITH.

- Be aware of imposter sources that pull you to counterfeit faith.

- Be an earnest contender of THE FAITH because them that are reprobate concerning THE FAITH are among us.

The LORD'S Purposes

Counsel. Advice. Purpose. Plan.

See Below Referenced Scriptures.

- Luke 7:50
- Ephesians 3
- Acts 3:15
- 2 Timothy 3:8

Reprobate: Not standing the test, not approved unfit for. Unapproved, that is rejected; worthless (literally or morally) castaway, reprobate

Reference: Thayer/Strong's Definition

HAVE NOT BOWED THEIR KNEE TO BAAL

"I have left me seven thousand in Israel, all the knees which have not bowed unto Baal, and every mouth which hath not kissed him."

(I Kings 19:18) KJV

The Book of Revelation, twelfth chapter teaches us that "the dragon was wroth with the woman and went to make war with the remnant of her seed, which keep the commandments of God, and have the testimony of Jesus Christ."

To 'bow' your knee is to pay homage to.

As ambassadors of Christ, we are to worship our Father ONLY. The scripture teaches us to pray after this manner: "Our Father which art in heaven, Hallowed be thy name..." No other name is to be hallowed.

"*Surely I come quickly.*" Even so... Come, Lord Jesus.

May the grace of our Lord Jesus Christ be with you.

Amen.

Question:

In what way(s) have mankind bowed their knee to Baal?

The LORD'S Purposes

Counsel. Advice. Purpose. Plan.

See below referenced scriptures.

- Revelation 12
- Revelation 22:20-21

Dragon: a dragon, a great serpent, a name for Satan.

(Reference: Thayer Definition)

THE 'WHOSOEVER' WILL

"And it shall come to pass, that whosoever shall call on the name of the LORD shall be delivered: for in mount Zion and in Jerusalem shall be deliverance, as the LORD hath said, and in the remnant whom the LORD shall call."

(Joel 2:32) KJV

REMNANT: Survivor, remaining, rest.

(Reference: BDB/Strong's Definition)

LORD, who may dwell in your sanctuary? Who may live on Your holy hill?

- *He whose walk is blameless and does what is righteous*
- *He who speaks truth from his heart and has no slander on his tongue*
- *He who does his neighbor no wrong and cast no slur on his fellowman*
- *He who despises a vile man but honors those who fear the Lord*
- *He who keeps his oath even when it hurts*
- *He who lends money without usury (interest)*
- *He who does not accept a bribe against the innocent*

He who does these things will never be shaken.

Whosoever will, let him come. Many are called but few are chosen. We must lift up our soul and trust in the LORD our God. He will not let us be put to shame. He will not allow our enemies to triumph over us.

If our hope is in the LORD... WE WILL NOT BE PUT TO SHAME.

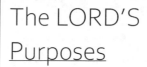

The LORD'S Purposes

Counsel. Advice. Purpose. Plan.

GOD EXPECTS PERSONAL ACCOUNTABILITY WORSHIP AND OBEDIENCE OUT OF ALL OF US.

See below referenced scriptures.

- Psalm 15
- Mark 8:34
- Matthew 22:14
- Psalm 25

- Sanctuary and holy hill are interchangeable words describing the focal point of Israelite worship – the dwelling place of God.

Reference: NIV

THE LIVING STONE AND A CHOSEN PEOPLE

"Therefore rid yourselves of all malice and all deceit, hypocrisy, envy, and slander of every kind. Like newborn babies, crave pure spiritual milk, so that by it you may grow up in your salvation, now that you have tasted that the Lord is good."

(2 Peter 2:1) NIV

Babies yearn to grow. Babies crave nourishment that will lead to growth. The Lord's chosen people are to (like newborn babies) crave pure spiritual milk that we may grow into maturity. That we may grow 'UP' in our salvation.

Jesus is the LIVING STONE. Rejected by men but chosen by God. Jesus is precious to God. And we, like living stones, are being built into a spiritual house.

- Being built to be a holy priesthood
- Offering spiritual sacrifices acceptable to God through Jesus Christ

"For in Scripture it says: See, I lay in Zion a chosen and precious cornerstone..."

Jesus is the precious Stone that the builders rejected. And if we trust in Him, we will never be put to shame.

We are a chosen people, a people belonging to God. A royal priesthood. A chosen nation. We proclaim the praises of Him who called us out of darkness into his marvelous light.

We are the people of God, and we receive mercy.

Thank you Father! ♥

The LORD'S Purposes

Counsel. Advice. Purpose. Plan.

See below referenced scriptures.

- 2 Peter 2:4-10

To those who do not believe, the Stone the builders rejected, has become a Stone that causes men to stumble and fall because they disobey the message.

WORD FIND

A	D	C	F	G	U	T	W	B	S	C	X	U	M	Z	F
L	P	O	S	I	T	I	O	N	A	V	L	T	A	G	B
O	B	E	D	I	E	N	T	R	S	Z	F	M	F	L	P
R	I	N	T	E	R	C	E	S	S	I	O	N	I	U	N
D	B	E	B	C	H	T	L	W	I	U	P	T	W	H	O
J	W	D	V	G	O	I	Q	T	G	E	V	J	U	A	T
E	*W*	*A*	*T*	*C*	*H*	*M*	*A*	*N*	N	T	H	Q	F	Y	V
H	S	C	L	I	A	I	M	S	M	W	P	K	D	A	Z
O	P	U	X	L	K	N	X	A	E	O	C	B	I	O	N
V	I	J	R	N	P	G	U	C	N	R	L	L	S	V	P
A	R	W	O	R	S	H	I	P	T	D	I	R	C	R	S
H	I	X	D	E	E	M	V	O	P	O	M	C	E	W	H
E	T	Y	O	P	L	N	L	B	M	F	A	E	R	I	Q
G	U	H	E	E	Y	D	D	L	V	G	T	K	N	M	Y
F	A	F	Q	N	W	A	H	E	T	O	E	M	Y	T	B
S	L	E	R	T	Z	P	K	P	R	D	Z	K	I	C	S
J	M	O	Q	K	Q	I	O	S	U	N	O	E	D	N	W
G	I	P	D	C	A	G	J	O	E	S	X	W	P	X	J
R	Z	H	N	J	H	E	D	G	E	R	L	S	D	Z	A

D. Burnette©

WATCHMAN	TIMING
LORD JEHOVAH	OBEDIENT
SPIRITUAL	SURRENDER
CLIMATE	REPENT
WALL	GOSPEL
TRUE	COMMANDMENTS
POSITION	HEDGE
WORD OF GOD	INTERCESSION
WORSHIP	ASSIGNMENT
DISCERN	

KNOWLEDGE CHECK:

1. Describe the prevailing climate as you perceive it.

2. What is the Kingdom of God?

3. What is the Kingdom of Heaven?

4. Who is the Remnant?

PRAYER TIME:

(A prayer point can be given to individuals, or one designated person.)

- **Father, Let Your will be done in earth as it is in heaven.**

- **Father, Be it unto me... as Your Word says.**

- **Father, We/I give Your Name the honor and glory that is due IT!**

- **Father, Restore Your Watchman to position.**

- **Establish your own prayer points...**

SECTION 2

What is a Watchman?

WHAT IS A WATCHMAN

NOTES: At A Quick Glance:	**GODS VESSEL** • **Chosen** • **Anointed** *"He said to me, "Son of man, stand up on your feet and I will speak to you." As he spoke, the Spirit came into me and raised me to my feet, and I heard him speaking to me."* *(Ezekiel 2:1)* NIV
	WATCHMAN: To look out or about, spy, keep watch, observe, behold, to peer into the distance, await, wait for (Reference: BDB Definition)
	The WATCHMAN is appointed by God for a 'specific' work. Or I will say… a 'specific' POSITION, in HIS Kingdom. When the Lord gives you a specific work, that involves your specific position in HIS Kingdom, do the work with all diligence, and with all your might. Your already have 'built' in you what it takes to accomplish the call on your life. No clarity… No clearance. WAIT ON CLARITY.

CHOSEN

- **"Son of man, stand up on your feet."**

Son of man:

Son, male child, Children (male and female)
Man, mankind, human being, of low degree, person

Stand:

To stand, remain, endure, take one's stand

Stand:

Abide (behind), appoint, arise, cease, confirm, continue, dwell, be employed, endure, establish, stand (fast, firm, still, up) tarry

(Reference: BDB/Strong's Definition)

- **"And I will speak to you."**

Speak:

To speak, declare, converse, command, promise, warn, threaten, sing

Speak:

To arrange, to subdue, answer, appoint, bid, command, commune, declare, destroy, give, name, promise, pronounce, rehearse, say, speak, be spokesman, talk, teach, tell, think

(Reference: BDB/Strong's Definition)

Watchman...

Generations are depending on you. Lives are on the line.

What is a Watchman?

Look Out. Keep. Watch. Observe.

NOTES:

ANOINTED

- **"The Spirit came into me and raised me to my feet."**

As the LORD spoke to Ezekiel, the Spirit came 'into' him. The Spirit empowered Ezekiel for the call.

It was necessary for the Spirit to come into Ezekiel, for the EQUIPPING and QUALIFYING.

The Spirit is who 'allows' the LORD's servant to stand (raised me to my feet) as a qualified servant.

- **"And I heard Him speak to me."**

As a Watchman, we are to submit under the Mighty Hand of God our Creator. We are to be open and obedient.

As Watchmen, we do not know everything, but we are however to remain and dwell in the posture that directs our 'whole' existence unto the Lord to be used.

When the Lord speaks to us, pay attention and proceed in the 'faith' that what the Lord has said will come to pass.

The Watchman is to follow discernment as a cookie crumb, and use discerning insight as clues to 'sustain' you, and to propel you into the/your next step. Your next move.

Definition

_____

_____

Clue:

Something that guides through an intricate procedure or maze of difficulties; specifically a piece of evidence that leads one toward the solution of a problem.

(Reference: Merriam Webster Online)

What is a Watchman?

Look Out. Keep. Watch. Observe.

NOTES:

NOTES: At A Quick Glance:	**GIVE 'WARNING' FROM THE LORD** • **A Prophet Has Been Among Them.** *"Son of man, I have made you a watchman for the house of Israel; so hear the word I speak and give them warning from me."* *(Ezekiel. 3:17)* NIV
	WARNING: To admonish, warn, teach, shine, send out light, be light, be shining, to gleam, enlighten (by caution) admonish, give warning (Reference: BDB/Strong's Concordance) ***Gleam:*** Shine brightly, especially with reflected light A faint or brief light, especially one reflected from something *Synonyms: Shine, glitter, glimmer, glow, spark* (Reference: Dictionary.com)
	Warning from the Lord: "When I say to a wicked man, 'You will surely die,' and you do not warn him or speak out to dissuade him from his evil ways in order to save his life, that wicked man will die for his sin, and I will hold you accountable for his blood. But if you do warn the wicked man and he does not turn from his wickedness or from his evil ways, he will die for his sin; but you will have saved yourself." *(Ezekiel 3:18-19)* NIV

A PROPHET HAS BEEN AMONG THEM

- **Whether they listen or fail to listen:**

"And whether they will listen or fail to listen-for they are a rebellious house-they will know that a prophet has been among them."

(Ezekiel 2:5) NIV

Rebellious: Bitter, bitterness, rebel

(Reference: Strong's Definition)

Often times the people the LORD send you to as a Watchman, will be 'obstinate and stubborn'. The people will rebel and not listen to you. Many people are obstinate and stubborn and hold tightly to their idols, traditions, ancestor persuasions, and mindsets.

Obstinate: Hard, cruel, stiff of neck, hard hearted

Stubborn: Rebel, turn away, backsliding, withdrew

(Reference: BDB/Strong's Definition)

You must still proclaim what the Lord has instructed.

- **They will know that a prophet has been among them:**

1 Samuel 3:19-20

What is a Watchman?

Look Out. Keep. Watch. Observe.

See Ezekiel 3:11

We are to go in the name of the Lord and speak to who we are sent to. We are to say to them... "This is what the Sovereign Lord says," whether they listen or fail to listen.

"When all this comes true-and it surely will-they will know that a prophet has been among them."

(Ezekiel 33:33) NIV

NOTES: At A Quick Glance:	**FOREHEAD WILL BE LIKE THE HARDEST STONE.** **'FLINT'** • **The Lord's Standard** • **No Compromise** • **Separating the Holy from the Profane** *"For the LORD GOD will help me; therefore shall I not be confounded: therefore have I set my face like a flint, and I know that I shall not be ashamed."* *(Isaiah 50:7)* KJV
	Confounded: To be humiliated. To insult. Blush. Be Ashamed. Reproached. Dishonored. To Wound. Taunt *Flint:* Flint. Rock. (In the sense of hardness) (Reference: BDB/Strong's Concordance)
	Forehead like flint. In Ezekiel 3rd chapter the LORD warns that Israel is a rebellious house. However... • The LORD will make the Watchman's face strong against their faces; and the Watchman's forehead strong against their foreheads. • The LORD instructs HIS Watchmen to fear them not, nor to be dismayed at their looks.

THE LORD'S STANDARD

"And might not be as their fathers, a stubborn and rebellious generation: a generation that set not their heart aright, and whose spirit was not steadfast with God."

(Psalm 78:8) KJV

Memories of our GOD, Jehovah Elohim, and HIS faithfulness helps and sustains generations. These memories and testimonies help to build and sustain FAITH.

Our FAITH in Jehovah's capabilities and trustworthiness is strengthened in our times of goodness and troubles because we foster relationship with HIM and HIS Supremacy.

The FAITHFULNESS of Jehovah is supposed to be passed down through the generations. The 'praiseworthy' stories of HIS SPLENDOR and AWESOMENESS is to be passed down to comfort us, and remind generations of HIS... POWER, LOVE, and PROTECTION. Thoughts of GOD prompts us to put away our doubts and distress and TRUST HIS WAY and STANDARD.

Instead, in many cases, the LORD's chosen people (the Children of Israel) have rebelled and have not been faithful to the Covenant in which the LORD established with our Father Abraham. The Children of Israel have hidden things of old, that was learned and heard about the LORD, and have rebelled and hardened their hearts.

What is a Watchman?

Look Out. Keep. Watch. Observe.

See Psalm 78:10-11

They did not keep God's covenant. They refused to live by God's law. They forgot what He had done for them, they forgot the wonders God had shown them.

Rebellion is as the sin of witchcraft, and stubbornness is as iniquity and idolatry.

Our people are in captivity. The house of Israel is in a state of rebellion. The children of Israel do not hearken unto the voice of the LORD's Prophets, because they do not hearken unto the voice of the LORD Himself. The children of Israel is impudent and hardhearted.

Impudent: Strong (usually in a bad sense. Hard. Bold. Violent.) Severe. Sharp. Hot. Stiff. Sore.

Hardhearted: Hard. Cruel. Obstinate. Difficult. Fierce. Intense. Stiff-necked. Rigorous (of battle) Stubborn. Heavy. Sorrowful. In trouble.

(Reference: BDB/Strong's Definition)

The Children of Israel...

- Walked after the imagination of their own heart, and after Baalim which their fathers taught them.

- Obeyed not, nor inclined their ear. Walked in the imagination of their evil heart. (*The LORD will therefore bring upon them all the words of this covenant, which He commanded them to do; but they did them not.*)

- This evil people, which refuse to hear my words, which walk in the imagination of their heart, and walk after other gods, to serve them, and to worship them, shall even be as this girdle, which is good for nothing. (Jer. 13:10) KJV

- Done worse than their fathers; and did walk every one after the imagination of his evil heart, and did not hearken unto the LORD.

What is a Watchman?

Look Out. Keep. Watch. Observe.

See Below Referenced Scriptures.

- 1 Samuel 15:23
- Ezekiel 3:7
- Jeremiah 9:14
- Jeremiah 11:8
- Jeremiah 16:12

27

NO COMPROMISE

They say still unto them that despise me, The LORD hath said, Ye shall have peace; and they say unto every one that walketh after the imagination of his heart, No evil shall come upon you.

(Jeremiah 23:17) KJV

The generations incline not their ear to hear the LORD'S instruction, but instead walk in their own counsels. Generations are walking in the imagination of their evil hearts and are going backward and not forward. Divine Revelation from the LORD is being ignored.

The faces of the generations are stubborn, hard and firm. Their imaginations are filled with lust. Evil and wretched are they.

Watchmen on the Wall, there is to be no compromise on your part. You must stand and speak what you are commanded to speak.

Watchman on the Wall, you cannot say Peace... when there is no peace. You cannot say unto them that walk after the imagination of their heart, that no evil will come upon them.

There is to be NO COMPROMISE.

We are not to accept standards that are lower than the LORD of Host's commands.

Question:

In what ways have you noticed compromise among Watchmen?

What is a Watchman?

Look Out. Keep. Watch. Observe.

See Below Referenced Scriptures.

- Jeremiah 7:24

SEPARATING THE HOLY FROM THE PROFANE

"Neither shall you profane my holy name, but I will be hallowed among the children of Israel: I am the LORD which hallowed you."

(Leviticus 22:32) KJV

The LORD is a Holy Sanctuary. A sacred place. The LORD is HOLY and the profane thing the LORD rejects.

Throughout Biblical history the children of Israel defiled their right-standing before Jehovah by profaning the things that the LORD had made Holy.

Even in this current dispensation, the children of Israel is in a state of defilement before our Father. Thus a state of being rejected by our Father. (There is a remnant (first-fruit) that has been preserved.) The children of Israel must turn from their wickedness and perverse ways and be restored.

The LORD will sanctify His great NAME, which was profaned among the heathen. The heathen will know that the LORD is LORD.

The LORD is merciful in that He calls His children from darkness into His marvelous LIGHT.

As Watchmen, we must be diligent to walk upright before He who called us to be a Watchman. We must walk in sanctification before Him, and keep that which is holy separated from the profane things.

What is a Watchman?

Look Out. Keep. Watch. Observe.

See Below Referenced Scriptures.

- Ezekiel 36:23

WHO IS A WATCHMAN

NOTES: At A Quick Glance:	**PROPHET WITH A (STRICT) ASSIGNMENT** • **Go in the Name of the Lord** • **Speak what the Lord tells you to speak** • **Rebellion not tolerated**
	Strict: Demanding that rules concerning behavior are obeyed and observed (Reference: Dictionary Online)
	Strict assignment: What is YOUR strict assignment(s) from the LORD?

GO IN THE NAME OF THE LORD

"Say to them, This is what the Sovereign LORD says..."

(Ezekiel 2:4) NIV

When the Lord gives you a CALL/MESSAGE, you MUST BELIEVE and walk in the *confidence* that the Lord is with you. The Lord is near and has provided all that you need to accomplish that which He places before you.

You will have to fight through the/YOUR feelings of inadequacy, feelings of lack of training, and concerns of lack of experience. When and what the Lord CALL's you to, believe this... the Lord has already trained and prepped YOU with the experience needed to accomplish the/YOUR assignment.

Assignments are 'assigned' by the Lord to an individual WATCHMAN'S responsibility, or care. The instruction is given by the Lord. And for the Lord's PURPOSES. Do not be deceived.

Be careful to discern imposter's who want to pimp out YOUR gifting to further their own agenda's.

[Many people are coming in the vein of 'Spiritism' and is engaging the spirit realm illegally. They hear and see, but their hearing and seeing is polluted and defiled. They are profane. Mixing the profane with the Holy Thing.]

Exercise YOUR discernment to know the holy from the profane. To know them that come in the name of THE LIE.

Your: Of, belonging to, or associated with you.

(Reference: FreeDictionary.com)

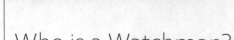

Who is a <u>Watchman?</u>

<u>Look Out. Keep. Watch. Observe.</u>

NOTES:

SPEAK WHAT THE LORD TELLS YOU TO SPEAK

"You must speak my words to them, whether they listen, for they are rebellious."

(Ezekiel 2:7) NIV

Watchman you must speak what the LORD gives you to speak. The LORD has trained you for such a time as this.

- You are a skilled soldier <u>prepared</u> to do THE WORK.
- You are <u>not to be afraid</u> of what they say. Nor be terrified by them. Or their words.
- Though you are among thorns and briars and you live among scorpions... <u>YOU ARE NOT TO BE AFRAID</u>.

You must speak to the rebellion, and not rebel like the rebellious house. You must open your mouth and eat what the LORD gives you.

They will know that a Prophet has been among them.

QUESTIONS:

Who is a <u>Watchman</u>?

<u>Look Out. Keep. Watch. Observe.</u>

See Below Referenced Scriptures.

- Ezekiel 2:6
- Ezekiel 2:8

REBELLION NOT TOLERATED

"The LORD was with Samuel as he grew up, and he let none of his words fall to the ground. And all Israel from Dan to Beersheba recognized that Samuel was attested as a prophet of the LORD."

(1 Samuel 3:19-20) NIV

Samuel was 'FAITHFUL.' The LORD continued to appear to him. Samuel was obedient and observed the voice of the LORD.

Samuel's obedience kept him in good standing with our Father.

Presumptuous Prophet

"But the prophet which shall presume to speak a word in my name which I have not commanded him to speak, or that shall speak in the name of other gods, even that prophet shall die."

(Deuteronomy 18:20) KJV

You, my fellow Watchman is God's spokesperson. You are a speaker for the LORD. Be VERY CAUTIOUS to not fall into presumption.

Presume: To boil up, seethe, act proudly, act presumptuously, act rebelliously, be arrogant, be rebelliously proud.

Presume: Be proud, deal proudly, presume, (come) presumptuously.

(Reference: BDB/Strong's Definition)

Who is a <u>Watchman?</u>

<u>Look Out. Keep. Watch. Observe.</u>

NOTES: At A Quick Glance:	**A 'DISTINCT' CALL/MAKE FROM GOD HIMSELF** • **"so hear the word I speak"** • **Consequences of 'your' disobedience** *"At the end of seven days the word of the Lord came to me: "Son of man, I have made you a watchman for the house of Israel; so hear the word I speak and give them warning from me."* *(Ezekiel 3:18)* NIV
	Distinct: Distinguishable to the eye or mind as being discreet. Not the same (Reference: Webster's Online)
	A distinct call from God. YOU are made to do what YOU do.

"SO HEAR THE WORD I SPEAK"

- **So hear the word I speak:**

The Lord Himself gives the Word and opens the ear of his servant to hear. The Lord's Word will be undeniable. You may doubt it, but it will be undeniable. The Lord speaks with clarity and precision and you will KNOW His voice. You will **KNOW** that the Lord has spoken.

You are to hear the Word of the LORD TO YOU, and walk under Jehovah's authority and fulfill what has been given you.

YOUR accountability is YOUR quality.
YOUR quality is YOUR accountability.

YOUR accountability will be exemplified in YOUR quality.

YOUR quality will be exemplified in YOUR accountability.

After a personal encounter with God, you will never be the same.

Accountability: The state of being accountable, meaning responsible for something or obligated to answer to someone, such as a person with more authority.

Quality: A special, distinctive, or essential character

(Reference: Webster Online)

The Watchman's <u>Call</u>

<u>Bestow. Make. To Be Put Upon.</u>

Walk under Jehovah's authority.

CONSEQUENCES OF 'your' DISOBEDIENCE

"...and I will hold you accountable for his blood."

(Ezekiel 3:18) NIV

Disobedience: Failure or refusal to obey rules by someone in authority. Lack of obedience or refusal to comply, disregard or transgression.

(Reference: Online Dictionary, Webster Online)

My fellow Watchman, lives are on the line. Your obedience or disobedience does not only <u>a</u>ffect the person you are instructed to engage, but it also will <u>e</u>ffect YOU.

The LORD will hold your disobedience to your charge. The person's blood will the LORD require at your hand.

Affect: Have an effect on; make a difference to.

Effect: A change which is a result or consequence of an action or other cause.

Remember Jonah In The Belly Of The Whale

The story of Jonah is a reminder to the Prophet/Watchman to not fall into self-righteousness or rebellion.

The LORD gave Jonah a Word to go to the city of Nineveh and preach against it because of its wickedness. Jonah was to warn the city of impending judgement if it did not repent.

Instead of initially obeying, Jonah ran the other way.

But how many of you know... that you can run... but you cannot hide from the LORD. He see you. Even while you are running.

The Watchman's <u>Call</u>

<u>Bestow. Make. To Be Put Upon.</u>

NOTES:

Jonah was met with the pit. The BELLY OF THE WHALE.

- Jonah from the belly of the whale (distress) called to the LORD

- Jonah acknowledged that he had been cast away into the deep

- Jonah acknowledged that the <u>LORD</u> had cast him away

- Jonah relied on the grace and mercy of the LORD to restore him

- Jonah looked again toward the Lord's Holy Temple, although the engulfing water threatened him and the deep surrounded him. And seaweed wrapped around his head.

Jonah was in disobedience, however, he came to his senses and repented before the LORD. The LORD brought Jonah's life up from the pit.

The LORD commanded the whale/pit to vomit Jonah out.

Hallelujah! The LORD is GOOD and MERCIFUL! REJOICE!!

The LORD heard Jonah's prayer.

Jonah came to realize that... "*those who cling to worthless idols forfeits the grace that could be theirs.*"

Jonah determined to make good on the vow. Jonah realized that salvation comes from the LORD.

The Word of the LORD came to Jonah a second time. This time Jonah obeyed.

Jonah declared the Word of the LORD to Nineveh. And because the Ninevites believed God, they declared a fast, put on sackcloth, and called urgently upon the LORD.

The Watchman's <u>Call</u>

<u>Bestow. Make. To Be Put Upon.</u>

See Below Referenced Scriptures.

- Jonah 2
- Jonah 3

The LORD in return had compassion and turned the judgement that He had threatened upon Nineveh.

Jonah, did not think the city of Nineveh was worthy of pardon, so Jonah became angry with the LORD for showing compassion.

Thought...

Was it maybe because Jonah was trying to save his own reputation and wanted the words he had spoken to Nineveh to come to pass? Could Jonah deep down had been a people-pleaser or tormented by self-pride?

Jonah prayed to the LORD and complained that he was angry enough to die.

The LORD asked Jonah... *"Have you any right to be angry?"*

Fellow Watchman, be very careful not to fall into the 'spirit' of Jonah.

The LORD showed great mercy on Jonah and delivered him from the belly of the whale/pit. However, Jonah did not feel that Nineveh was worthy of the same compassion.

How many of us have been forgiven much?

Remember that the LORD extends His compassion to whosoever HE wills.

You are merely a vessel being used to do the LORD's bidding. A vessel that needs/needed redemption just like the next man/woman.

The Watchman's Call

<u>Bestow. Make. To Be Put Upon.</u>

See Below Referenced Scriptures.

- Jonah 4:9

YOUR THOUGHTS ON JONAH's MOTIVE(S)?

_____

_____

_____

"If at any time I announce that a nation or kingdom is to be uprooted, torn down and destroyed, and if that nation I warned repents of its evil, then I will relent and not inflict on it the disaster I had planned.

And if at another time I announce that a nation or kingdom is to be built up and planted, and if it does evil in my sight and does not obey me, then I will reconsider the good that I had intended to do for it.

(Jeremiah 18: 7-10) NIV

NOTES: At A Quick Glance:	**NO MAN CAN 'APPOINT' YOU (LEGALLY)** • **Known you from the womb** • **"I have made you a watchman"** *By thee have I been holden up from the womb: thou art he that took me out of my mother's bowels: my praise shall be continually of thee."* *(Psalm 71:6)* KJV
	APPOINT: Assign a job or role to someone ***Made:*** Made or formed in a particular place or by a particular process. (Reference: Online Dictionary)
	No man can appoint you, nor anoint you to be a Watchman.

KNOWN YOU FROM THE WOMB

"As thou knowest not what is the way of the spirit, nor how the bones do grow in the womb of her that is with child: even so thou knowest not the works of God who maketh all."

(Ecclesiastes 11:5) KJV

RIGHTEOUS SEED:

Your journey and your course of life has and is always being molded by the Potter. You are the clay.

Our Father made us and formed us from our mother's womb. The LORD is our Redeemer, and He makes all things.

The Potter has power over the clay. The Potter is shaping us all to be vessels of honor.

We are to hearken unto the voice of our GOD. We are the House of Jacob. The Remnant of the House of Israel. We are upheld by the LORD from conception, (the womb) and are carried by the LORD from birth. (Formed and molded into vessels of honor.)

The Lord supports, sustains, assists, holds up, and furnishes us.

Before the LORD formed you in the belly, the LORD knew you. Before you came out of the womb, the LORD sanctified you and ordained you a Prophet unto the nations. (See Jeremiah 1:5)

The LORD separated you from your mother's womb, and called you by His grace.

WICKED SEED:

"The wicked are estranged from the womb: they go astray as soon as they be born, speaking lies.
Their poison is like the poison of a serpent: they are like the deaf adder that stoppeth her ear." (Psalm 58:3-4) KJV

The Watchman's Call

<u>Bestow. Make. To Be Put Upon.</u>

See Below Referenced Scriptures.

- Jeremiah 18
- Isaiah 44:24
- Isaiah 46:3
- Galatians 1:15

I HAVE MADE YOU A WATCHMAN

"At the end of seven days the word of the Lord came to me: "Son of man, I have <u>made you a</u> <u>watchman</u> for the house of Israel; so hear the word I speak and give them warning from me."

(Ezekiel 3:18) KJV

<u>God shapes the character of the Watchman to fit his mission:</u>

- The Lord will make you as unyielding and hardened as they are.
- The LORD will make your forehead harder than flint
- DO NOT BE AFRAID OF THEM. Though they are a rebellious house.
- Hear the Word from the LORD.
- SPEAK
- Give warning from the LORD.

QUESTIONS:

The Watchman's <u>Call</u>

<u>Bestow. Make. To Be Put Upon.</u>

See Below Referenced Scriptures.

- Ezekiel 3: 8-9

NOTES: At A Quick Glance:	**YOU HAVE EATEN THE /ROLL-SCROLL (THE WORD OF GOD)**
	• **Roll-Scroll (The Word of God)** • **Meditated on/Digested** *And he said to me, "Son of Man, eat what is before you, eat this scroll; then go and speak to the house of Israel" So I opened my mouth, and he gave me the scroll to eat.* *(Ezekiel 3:1-2)* NIV *Moreover he said unto me, Son of man, eat that thou findest; eat this roll, and go speak unto the house of Israel. So I opened my mouth and he caused me to eat that roll.* *(Ezekiel 3:1-2)* KJV
	Roll: Roll, book, writing, volume (Reference: BDB/Strong's Definition)
	The Lord will unroll it before you.

ROLL-SCROLL/THE WORD OF GOD

Some translations say roll. Some translations say scroll.

We are to eat what the LORD gives us and not be as the rebellious house in which he sends us too.

The Word of the LORD makes us strong and wise. We are to consume/digest the message. We are to eat the roll-scroll put before us. Ezekiel ate God's message and found God's message (spiritual food) good and sweet as honey.

The message the Lord gives you is the LORDS WORDS to give to the people. The LORDS WORDS is what <u>will</u> have POWER. We are to speak with the LORDS WORDS.

We are to cause our belly to eat, and our bowels to be filled with the roll-scroll the Lord give us.

Belly: Belly, womb, body. As a seat of mental faculties

Bowels: Internal organs, inward parts, intestines, belly, place of emotions, distress or love (figuratively)

Mouth: (As organ of speech) opening, orifice (of a well)

(Reference: BDB/Strong's Definition)

The message the Lord's gives us is WHAT WE WERE PUT HERE ON EARTH TO SPEAK. Mankind is not doing God a 'favor' by obeying, worshipping and reverencing Him. It is what we are on this earth to do.

We are created for the Lord's glory.

Always remember, the Lord can raise up a stone to cry out for Him.

The Watchman's Message

<u>Speech. Word. Utterance. Work.</u>

See Below Referenced Scriptures.

- Ezekiel 2:8
- Ezekiel 3:1-3
- Ezekiel 3:4
- Isaiah 3:7
- Matthew 3:9

On both sides written words of lament and mourning and woe.

Ezekiel 2:9-10

A Watchman's template or social fabric is the WORD of GOD. This is like a number find.

You cannot legally get to the number 2 unless you start with the number 1. Then you must access the numbers two, three, four, and five (in order) to get to the number six.

I say legally, because unless you enter in by the door (Jesus Christ) then you are illegally accessing spiritual terrain. And when illegally assessed, there is danger. This is where the thief has legal right to steal, kill and destroy. BE WARNED!

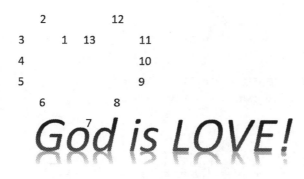

D. Burnette©

The Watchman's Message

Speech. Word. Utterance. Work.

NOTES:

MEDITATED ON/DIGESTED

"But his delight is in the law of the LORD; and in his law doth he meditate day and night."

(Psalm 1:2) KJV

Meditate: To moan, growl, utter, muse, mutter, meditate, devise, plot, speak, imagine, study, talk.

(Reference: BDB/Strong's Definition)

Watchman/Watchmen, we are to take the Word of the Lord to heart before giving it to others. The Word of the Lord must be our desire. Our longing. Our good pleasure. The Word of the Lord must be a valuable thing in our OWN life.

The Lord's Word must be deep in our hearts and show in our OWN actions and life before we can effectively help others understand and apply the gospel. The GOOD NEWS of Christ.

We must feed OURSELVES spiritually just as we do physically. We cannot just glance at the Word of God; we must instead meditate on it. We must digest the Word. We must take care to make the Word of the Lord a daily part of our OWN lives.

The Lord's voice must become 1st nature to us. Even above our own voice. Our own thoughts and perceptions. We must be careful to follow the voice of the Lord.

The voice of another you will not follow.

Your words are being depended upon for accuracy. And your accuracy is only as good as your QUALITY of hearing the Word of the Lord.

This is serious business. Lives are on the line.

The Watchman's Message

<u>Speech. Word. Utterance. Work.</u>

NOTES:

NOTES: At A Quick Glance:	**YOU HAVE RECEIVED A 'CLEAR' WORD/THEME** • **"I am "sending" you to..."** *"And he said unto me, Son of man, I send thee to the children of Israel, to a rebellious nation that hath rebelled against me: they and their fathers have transgressed against me, even unto this day."* *(Ezekiel 2: 3 (8))* KJV
	clarity: The quality of being certain or definite (Reference: Online Dictionary)

IF and WHEN you have received a message, and have been given commission from the LORD, then you have received clarity.

Not the 'whole' per se, because we prophesy in part. However, you 'know' direction. You have a Vision (a message) to follow/be led by.

DO NOT ALLOW ANYONE TO EDIT THE CLEAR WORD THAT YOU HAVE RECEIVED FROM THE LORD.

If you are in the stage(s) of receiving instruction and direction, the LORD may use another to confirm, however; they <u>will</u> <u>not</u> change your message.
The LORD doesn't need anyone else's help.
As a Watchman, the LORD (The Potter) has made you into a vessel programmed to receive from HIM.
A Watchman is developed to be Mature in the LORD.

BE WARNED! 🏛

"I am sending you to…"

"At the end of seven days the word of the Lord came to me: "Son of man, I have made you a watchman for the house of Israel; so hear the word I speak and give them warning from me."

(Ezekiel 3:17) KJV

<u>Give them warning from me:</u>

"This is what the LORD says: Stand in the courtyard of the LORD'S house and speak to all the people of the towns of Judah who come to worship in the house of the LORD. <u>Tell</u> them everything I command you; do not <u>omit</u> a word. Perhaps they will listen and each will <u>turn</u> from his evil way. Then I will <u>relent</u> and not bring on them the disaster I was planning because of the evil they have done.

Say to them, 'This is what the LORD says: If you do not listen to me and follow my <u>law</u>, which I have set before you, and if you do not listen to the words of my servants the prophets, whom I have sent to you again and again (though you have not listened), then I will make this house like Shiloh and this city an object of <u>cursing</u> among all the nations of the earth."

(Jeremiah 26: 2-6) NIV

Prophets oppose idolatrous lifestyles and faulty foundations. Prophets are often times looked at as traitors and rebels. Evil systems will try and discredit the Prophets voice.

You are to stand anyhow. The LORD, who you fight for, will avenge you.

The Watchman's Message

<u>Speech. Word. Utterance. Work.</u>

See Below Referenced Scriptures.

TELL:

- Jeremiah 1:17
- Matthew 28:20
- Acts 20:27

Omit:

- Deuteronomy 4:2

Turn:

- Jeremiah 36:7

Relent:

- Jeremiah 18:8

Listen:

- Leviticus 28:14

Law:

- 1 Ki 9:6

Shiloh:

- Jos 18:1

Cursing:

- 2 Ki 22:19

NOTES: At A Quick Glance:	
	### YOU 'BECOME' ALIGNED AND ACCLIMATED TO THE MESSAGE you CARRY • **But When I Speak, I Will Open Your Mouth** *"Moreover he said unto me, Son of man, all thy words that I shall speak unto thee receive in thine heart, and hear with thine ears...."* *(Ezekiel 3:10)* KJV
	heart: Inner man, mind, will, heart, soul, as seat to appetites, emotions, and passions; as a seat of courage, understanding, inclination, the heart (as the most internal organ.) (Reference: BDB/Strong's Concordance)
	You become obedient to the voice of God. "And go, get thee to them of the captivity, unto the children of thy people, and speak unto them, and tell them, Thus saith the LORD GOD; whether they will hear, or whether they will forbear. Then the spirit took me up, and I heard behind me a voice of a great rushing, saying, Blessed be the glory of the LORD from his place." (Ezekiel 3:11-12) KJV

"BUT WHEN I SPEAK, I WILL OPEN your MOUTH"

"But when I speak with thee, I will open thy mouth, and thou shalt say unto them, Thus saith the Lord to warn the wicked from his wicked way, to save his life; ...

(Ezekiel 3:27) KJV

LIVES are on the line my fellow Watchman. It is crucial that we be in position to hear instruction. Not hearing because of our lack of preparation, is not a waiver of responsibility. Instead it leaves you with gallons of blood on your hands. BE WARNED.

In the book of Ezekiel chapter three we learn STRUCTURE and PROCESS. (verses 24-21)

- Go, shut thyself within thine house
- Thou shall not go out among them
- And I will make thy tongue cleave to the roof of thy mouth, and thou shalt be <u>dumb,</u> and shall not be a reprover: for they are a rebellious house
- But when I speak with thee, I will open thy mouth, and thou shalt say unto them, Thus saith the LORD to warn the wicked from his wicked way
- When you warn, you deliver your own soul

When the time presents itself, the Lord will open your mouth. You will then speak and be no more dumb. (Put to silence.)

You will be a sign unto them, and they shall know that the LORD is LORD.

The Watchman's Message

<u>Speech. Word. Utterance. Work.</u>

See Below Referenced Scriptures.

- Ezekiel 3:22-23
- Ezekiel 24:27
- Ezekiel 29:21

Dumb*:* Bind, be dumb, put to silence.

(Reference: Strong's Concordance)

"Son of man, say to the house of Israel, This is what you are saying: Our offenses and sins weigh us down, and we are wasting away because of them. How then can we live? Say to them, 'As surely as I live declares the Sovereign Lord, I take no pleasure in the death of the wicked, but rather that they turn from their ways and live. Turn! Turn from your evil ways! Why will you die, O house of Israel?'

(Ezekiel 33:10) NIV

THE WATCHMAN'S SANCTIFICATION

NOTES: At A Quick Glance:	**0bedience is 'MANDATORY'** • **Obedience is better than sacrifice** • **Rebellion is as THE SIN of witchcraft** • **Stubbornness is as iniquity and idolatry** *"Behold, to obey is better than sacrifice,* *and to hearken than the fat of rams."* *(1 Samuel 15:22)* KJV
	Obey: To hear, listen, understand, give heed, to consent ***Sacrifice:*** Offering, sacrifice of dead things (Reference: BDB Concordance)
	You disobey...there is a price to pay. Be warned. We must be diligent to hearken to the voice and instruction from the LORD. When we hearken we hear and we are attentive. Let us always give heed to and regard what we have heard from the LORD.

OBEDIENCE IS BETTER THAN SACRIFICE

Obedience is 'YOUR' duty. YOU MUST OBEY THE DIRECTIVES OF THE VOICE OF THE LORD.

Do not follow other voices. The Lord's sheep know HIS voice, and the voice of another, HIS sheep will not follow.

When you hear the voice of the LORD, submit yourselves and OBEY. The LORD will cause you to hear. So you are without excuse. When and/or if we fail to obey the LORD, it is/was not because we did not HEAR. It will be because the conscious choice was made to NOT OBEY.

We are the called of Jesus Christ. We are His Saints. Divinely selected and appointed. We are to be obedient to the faith among all nations.

Whom we yield ourselves servants to obey, that is who our master is. We are either servants of disobedience, (sin unto death); or we are servants of obedience. (Unto righteousness.)

We revenge all disobedience when our obedience is fulfilled. When we are obedient we are in a 'ready' stance. Prepared to raise the standard on disobedience.

Remember that through the disobedience of one, (Adam), many were made sinners. But... Thank the LORD that through one, (Christ's obedience), many shall be made righteous. Hallelujah.

Fellow Watchman, OBEY and HEARKEN to the voice of the LORD.

The Watchman's Sanctification

Consecration. Purification. Holiness. Purity.

See Below Referenced Scriptures.

- Romans 1:6
- Romans 1:5
- Romans 6:16
- 2 Corinthians 10:6
- Romans 5:19

REBELLION IS AS THE SIN OF WITCHCRAFT

"For rebellion is as the sin of witchcraft..."

(1 Samuel 15:23) KJV

Rebellion: Bitter(ness), revolt against Jehovah

Witchcraft: Divination (also including its fee), oracle – reward of divination, divine sentence, witchcraft

(Reference: BDB/Strong's Definition)

We must remain blameless before our God. The LORD raises His prophets up and the LORD puts His words in the prophet's mouth. The prophet tells the people what the LORD commands.

The nations listen to them who practice divination and sorcery and do those things that are not pleasing in the sight of our God.

We are not to learn to imitate the detestable practices of the nations.

We obey the LORD so that things will go well with us. The Lord has not permitted us to do as the nations. We are a peculiar people. A royal priesthood. In the world, but not of the world.

"When you enter the land the LORD your God is giving you, do not learn to imitate the detestable ways of the nations there. Let no one be found among you who sacrifices his son or daughter in the fire, who practices divination or sorcery, interprets omens, engages in witchcraft, or casts spells, or who is a medium or spiritist or who consults the dead."

(Deuteronomy 18: 9-11) NIV

The Watchman's Sanctification

Consecration. Purification. Holiness. Purity.

See Below Referenced Scriptures.

- Deuteronomy 19:18

STUBBORNESS IS AS INIQUITY AND IDOLATRY

"For rebellion is as the sin of witchcraft, and stubbornness is as iniquity and idolatry."

(1 Samuel 15:23) KJV

Stubbornness: To press, push, be insolent, display pushing (arrogance, presumption)

Iniquity: Trouble, wickedness, sorrow, idolatry, to exert oneself, usually in vain, strictly nothingness: affliction, evil, false, idol, mourners (-ing), unjust, unrighteous

Idolatry: Idolatry, idols, image(s), teraphim, family idol. (a.) a kind of idol used in household shrine or worship. A healer.

(Reference: BDB/Strong's Definition)

Stubborn as a mule.

Do you remember the phrase?

Being stubborn is as iniquity and idolatry.

BE WARNED.

QUESTIONS:

The Watchman's Sanctification

<u>Consecration. Purification. Holiness. Purity.</u>

NOTES:

NOTES: At A Quick Glance:	**WORSHIP BEFORE THE LORD IS your 'POSTURE'** • **Worship in spirit and in truth** • **Looking for true worshippers (heart posture)** *"But the hour cometh, and now is, when the true worshippers shall worship the Father in spirit and in truth for the Father seeketh such to worship him."* *(John 4:23)* KJV
	Worship: To kiss the hand to (towards) one, in token of reverence, prostrate oneself in homage, adore. (Reference: Strong's Concordance)
	Worship is your heartbeat. You know that the LORD is worthy of the adoration… and YOU LIVE IT.

WORSHIP IN SPIRIT AND IN TRUTH

"God is a Spirit and they that worship Him must worship Him in spirit and in truth."

(John 4:24) KJV

Spirit: 1. The third person of the triune God, the Holy Spirit, coequal, coeternal with the Father and the Son

(a.) sometimes referred to in a way which emphasizes his personality and character (the Spirit)

(b,) sometimes referred to in a way which emphasizes his work and power (the Spirit)

2. The spirit, i.e. the vital principle by which the body is animated

(a.) the rational spirit, the power by which the human body feels, thinks, decides

(b) the soul

a current of air, that is breath (blast) or a breeze, God, Christ's spirit, the Holy spirit: -ghost, life, spirit (-ual, -ually), mind.

Spirit: The disposition or influence which fills and governs the soul of any one, breath of nostrils or mouth, a life giving spirit. Mind.

Truth: What is true in any matter under consideration, according to truth, respecting God and the execution of his purposes through Christ, and respecting the duties of man

(Reference: Thayer/Strong's Definition)

The Watchman's Sanctification

Consecration. Purification. Holiness. Purity.

The LORD expects personal obedience, worship, and truth.

LOOKING FOR TRUE WORSHIPPERS

"For the Father seeketh such to worship Him."

(John 4:23) KJV

Remember you are Special Op's (Operations). Your position is strategic and ON PURPOSE. And equally, your posture before the LORD is where your 'quality' is.

Your assignments are carried out through 'legal' engagement with the Spirit Realm. Worship is your MAJOR weapon. Worship grants you access to the Throne of God.

"But the LORD who brought you up out of the land of Egypt with great power and a stretched out arm, him shall ye fear, and him shall ye worship, and to him shall ye do sacrifice."

(2 Kings 17:36) KJV

Your worship stance is where the POWER is.

The LORD is seeking you out. The LORD is seeking out your WORSHIP to Him.

The LORD, whose name is Jealous, is a jealous God. He tells us to worship no other god. We must take heed that we be not deceived and turn aside to worship other gods.

"For they went and served other gods, and worshipped them, gods whom they knew not, and who he had not given unto them."

(Deuteronomy 29:26) KJV

The Watchman's Sanctification

Consecration. Purification. Holiness. Purity.

See Below Referenced Scriptures.

- Exodus 34:14
- Deuteronomy 11:16

THE WATCHMAN'S POSITION

NOTES: At A Quick Glance:	
	ON THE 'WALL' • **Elevated so that you can see/discern** • **Can be lonely and emotionally intense** *"And David sat between the two gates: <u>and the watchman **went** up to the</u> roof <u>over the gate</u> unto the wall, and lifted up his eyes, and looked, and behold a man running alone."* *(2 Samuel 18-24)* KJV
	Wall: Wall, meaning to join; a wall of protection, walled. (Reference: BDB/Strong's Concordance)
	The 'wall' is your strategic effective place. So that you can gaze and see. (perceive) See 2 Samuel 18: 24-27

ELEVATED SO YOU CAN SEE/DISCERN

"And the watchman cried, and told the king, And the king said, if he be alone, there is tidings in his mouth. And he came apace, and drew near.

(2 Samuel 18:25) KJV

"And the <u>watchman saw</u> another man running and <u>the watchman called unto the porter</u>, and <u>said</u>, Behold another man running alone. And the king said, He also bringeth tidings."

(2 Samuel 18:26) KJV

The Watchman **says'** what he/she SEE. (At the LORD'S <u>command</u>.)

The "SEEING" is an Anointing. A spiritual gifting that is graced upon the Watchman. The Watchman does not know HOW or WHY he/she SEE's what they SEE... The LORD knows and therefore supernaturally imposes the "Word of Wisdom" or "Word of Knowledge" into the perception of His Watchmen.

Watchman... WHO SHOULD already BE PROPERLY ALIGNED and IN SERVICE FOR USE.

"And there stood a watchman on the tower in Jezreel, and he **spied** the company of Jehu as he came, **and said, I see a company**. And Joram said, Take a horseman, and send to meet them, and let him say, Is it peace?"

(2 Kings 9:17) KJV

Spied: To see, look at, inspect, perceive, consider

Spied: Advise self, appear, approve, behold, consider, discern, have experience, gaze, take heed, perceive, spy, stare, surely, think, view, visions.

(Reference: BDB Definition)

The Watchman's Position

<u>Pose. Arrangement. Stance. Location.</u>

NOTES:

A Watchman's experience (discernment/senses exercised) is key. What is the Watchman saying?

In the book of second Kings ninth chapter verses nineteen through twenty, the watchman saw and spoke what he saw. What he perceived.

The Watchman's assessment of spiritual climate is a power move in the spirit realm. Watchmen are needed to spiritually and scripturally approve or disapprove, enforce standard, and/or to warn of impending danger.

ANY QUESTIONS?:

The Watchman's Position

**Pose. Arrangement.
Stance. Location.**

NOTES:

CAN BE LONELY AND EMOTIONALLY INTENSE

"Except the LORD build the house, they labor in vain that build it: except the LORD keep the city, the watchman walketh but in vain."

(Psalm 127:1) KJV

You may find yourself walking amongst those who are building in vain. Amongst them that 'keep their own city.' Them having a form of godliness but denying the power thereof.

The Lord's WORD is always POWERFUL, but not always POPULAR.

Therefore, the Watchman is not always accepted. The Watchman's perception is very finely tuned to true spiritual climate. The Watchman's perception is as a "spiritual forensic." In that the examining is always turned on; gathering data, separating the holy from the profane, casting down imaginations and every high thing exalting itself against the knowledge of God.

When the enemy comes in like a flood the Lord raises up a STANDARD. And when there is a watchman available, the imposing thing is spiritually detected/discerned, challenged/exposed (by reporting (what is perceived/seen) to the proper authority) and the STANDARD is enforced through the 'chain of command' working in tandem.

LONELY:

The wall is a "solo" stance. BUT YOU WERE CREATED TO ENDURE THE RIGORS of the waves of emotions, temptations/seductions, and mania that will present itself to you.

The Watchman's Position

Pose. Arrangement. Stance. Location.

NOTES:

EMOTIONAL INTENSE:

The Watchman is called by God. No man appoints a Watchman. Thus, this becomes spiritual friction between the Watchman and the appointed men/women in hierarchies that the spirit of religion/Mammon has established.

Jehovah Elohim's TRUE CHURCH (Ekklesia) will know HIS Voice, and the voice of another they will not follow...

Many Pharisees and Sadducees will buck against the Word that the LORD has given you to say.

And this in and of itself becomes a spiritual intensity likened to coming head-to-head with a stubborn bull that refuses to move.

Scenario...

You are on the 'good' path and all of a sudden, the opposing force(s) of darkness, rises up before you and challenges the very core of what you know to be TRUTH.

But because you the Watchman, is also 'unmovable' and steadfast in the work of the LORD, the spiritual standoff occurs.

The Kingdom of LIGHT against the Kingdom of Darkness.

No physical violence, however, in the spirit realm the violence is undeniable. And you will 'by force' battle the unseen realm operating through flesh and blood. And by the force and Power of the Holy Spirit, you, the Watchman will STAND. And the Kingdom of Light will advance.

Now this is not to be confused with carnal rebellion on your part, or "just having your own way" ... this is about an UNCIRCIMCISED GIANT DEFYING THE WORD OF THE LORD.

Because you have heard a Word from the Commander in Chief. (The LORD of Hosts) You have received a perception/Seeing from the Kingdom of Heaven and you cannot be MOVED from it. That's just how you are built. You are built GOD TOUGH.

The Watchman's Position

Pose. Arrangement. Stance. Location.

See Below Referenced Scriptures.

- 1 Corinthians 15:58
- Matthew 11:12

Like David boldly raised up against Goliath. Not in his own strength, but in a "movement of stealth" that raised a STANDARD against the kingdom of darkness and its roar.

That is what the intensity is.

YOU turn into another man/woman. The Lord has given you a new heart and spirit. You have the LORD'S spirit within you and this causes you to walk in the LORD's statues and judgements. You will do them. You are made to do them.

You cannot go back. You can't turn to the left or right (without falling into disobedience) The only right-standing option in that time and space of battle (whether it lasts another moment or another year) is to STAND and wait to see the SALVATION OF THE LORD regarding the thing that HE is raising the STANDARD against.

Everybody in the religious system is not necessarily an enemy of the LORD. Many are indoctrinated by doctrines of demons, and need prayer. Be careful to use discernment and proceed as necessary.

QUESTION:

1. **How do/did you handle emotional intensity?**

The Watchman's Position

Pose. Arrangement. Stance. Location.

See Below Referenced Scriptures.

- 1 Samuel 10:6
- Ezekiel 36:26-27

THE WATCHMAN'S POSITION: *Continued*

NOTES: At A Quick Glance:	**WHERE IS THE 'WALL'**
	• **Located in the spirit realm/spiritual climate** *"The burden of Dumah, He calleth to me out of Seir, Watchman, what of the night? Watchman, what of the night?"* *(Isaiah 21:11)* KJV
	Realm: A Kingdom. A field or domain of activity or interest (Reference: Online Definition)
	Isaiah twenty-one and six teaches us that Watchmen are set. And they declare what they see.

LOCATED IN THE SPIRIT REALM/ SPIRITUAL CLIMATE

A Watchman eyes':

Outwardly you see the natural. But your eyes inwardly are seeing the spiritual. Your eyes are gazing and scanning the spiritual climate.

"Eye be single"

Everything about you is a radar. You are a Bluetooth hotspot. You are connected to the frequency in your sphere of influence.

Everything is not your assignment. The LORD does not OVERLOAD a Watchman.

The LORD instead appoints/assigns a WALL to each Watchman.

The Watchman is prepped to successfully fulfil the mission of his WALL/Assignment(s). Even when you think you are not, you are. The Lord knows that you are capable. If you weren't the Lord would not give you the WALL/Assignment(s).

Your WALL/Assignment(s) remains fortified with the mortar/ clay of...

- **Intercession**
- **Warfare**
- **Praise & Worship**

The Watchman's Position

Pose. Arrangement. Stance. Location.

NOTES:

NOTES: At A Quick Glance:	**INTERCESSION, WARFARE, PRAISE & WORSHIP** • **Prayer life/Intercession** • **Whole Armor of God (Warfare)** • **An instrument of Praise & Worship**
	Intercession: The act of intervening on behalf of another *Warfare:* An expedition, campaign, military service *Praise:* Adoration, thanksgiving (paid to God) *Worship:* To bow down, humbly beseech (Reference: BDB/Strong's Concordance/Online Dictionary)
	The Watchman's 'Wall' is your strategic effective place. The 'Wall' is where you intercede, warfare, praise, worship, and watch. The Watchman's 'Wall' is where THE/your POWER is. The Watchman's 'Wall' can be likened to an electrical outlet. You MUST plug in. In order to receive and properly charge, you MUST plug in and be... *empowered/endowed/ anointed* <u>by</u> <u>THE</u> <u>SOURCE</u>. (Jehovah Elohim) You are not your own, always remember that you, as a Watchman, have been called, trained, and commissioned by <u>THE</u> <u>SOURCE</u>.

PRAYER LIFE/INTERCESSION

Intercession is YOUR powerful weapon. Prayer is essential. YOUR prayer life is essential. A Watchman is only as effective as his/her communication with the Lord. (Home base.)

YOUR prayer life/intercession, is where YOU, the Watchman, gets briefed.

Be mindful, that in intercession, it is not about the Watchman's personal prayer requests here. It is about the Watchman's "show up" to work. "Show up" to 'the work'. <u>YOU ARE ON DUTY</u>!

- Here you will repent if needed.
- Enter in to the Holy Place.
- Intercede/stand in the gap – Warfare
- Lay at the Lord's feet

Continue to faithfully pray. Your prayers are heard, but they may be challenged/hindered by unseen forces. Continue to pray and trust the Lord to answer in and at the right time.

The Lord will give you skill and understanding. Angels will be on assignment to work with you.

While Daniel was speaking, praying, confessing his sin, the sin of Israel; and presenting supplication before the Lord, Gabriel the angel showed up to give Daniel skill and understanding.

The angel called Daniel 'Greatly Beloved.'

Daniel humbled himself and set his heart to understand before the Lord. The Lord heard Daniel's words and the Lord responded to Daniel.

The Watchman's Position

<u>Pose. Arrangement. Stance. Location.</u>

See Below Referenced Scriptures.

- Daniel 10:12
- Daniel 9:23
- Daniel 9:21

Praying in the Holy Ghost is the fuel that propels you.

Remember, and stand on the confidences, that no weapon formed against you will prosper and every tongue rising against you in judgement, you can condemn. This is YOUR HERITAGE as servants of the Lord.

Stand In The Gap:

"And I sought a man among them that should make up the hedge and stand in the gap before me for the land, that I should not destroy it: but I found none." (Ezekiel 22:30) KJV

Watchman, in intercession, YOU are purposed and designed to stand in the gap for Israel. (Spiritual) God's chosen people. YOU are going before the Lord in His Courts.

Israel is blind and cannot defend themselves currently. So the Lord looks for YOU to make up the hedge and stand in the gap.

"Ye have not gone up unto the gaps, neither made up the hedge for the house of Israel to stand in the battle in the day of the LORD."

(Ezekiel 13:5) KJV

Your Words Are A Weapon:

Watchman, YOUR words are a weapon. A weapon that will help or hinder. Remember that death and life are in the power of YOUR tongue. And you will be held accountable for your utterances.

The Watchman will see when the Lord brings again Zion. Hallelujah! What an honor.

The Watchmen will lift up their voices together and sing. The Watchman will see eye to eye when Zion is redeemed.

The Watchman's Position

Pose. Arrangement. Stance. Location.

See Below Referenced Scriptures.

- Isaiah 43
- Isaiah 52:8

A Watchman's role is not happenstance and of no effect.

A Watchman is a STRATEGIC STRIKE.

YOU, the Watchman, is on assignment to, and for the house of Israel.

You have been redeemed. Your purpose is to be a vessel unto the Lord. You are to be witnesses that:

Before the Lord God there was 'NO' god formed. Neither will there be after Him. Apart from HIM there is no Savior. Salvation is of the Lord.

WHOLE ARMOR OF GOD (Warfare)

The Watchman's Position

<u>**Pose. Arrangement. Stance. Location.**</u>

See Below Referenced Scriptures.

- Jeremiah 51:20
- Jeremiah 50:25

"This charge I commit unto thee, son Timothy, according to the prophecies which went before on thee, that thou by them mightiest <u>war</u> a good warfare.

(1 Timothy 1:18) KJV

War: 1. To make a military expedition, to lead soldiers to war or to battle (spoken of a commander)

2. To do military duty, be on active service, be a soldier

3. To fight

To serve in a military campaign; figuratively to execute the apostolate (with its arduous duties and functions). To contend with carnal inclinations: - soldier. (go to) war (-fare)

(Reference: Thayer/Strong's Definition)

Paul spoke to Timothy regarding the mantel/mandate that he carried. A mantel/mandate that would include hardship and danger. A mantel/mandate that included warfare. Warfare came with the Call. Warfare came with the territory.

The LORD IS OUR BATTLE AXE:

The Lord is our Battle Axe. The Lord is our weapons of war. And <u>with</u> <u>the</u> <u>Lord</u>, *we* *will* break in pieces the nations and destroy kingdoms.

Battle axe: War, club, hammer, smiter, battle axe

(Reference: BDB/Strong's Definition)

In days of old when the battles were physically fought by the Power of the Lord, the Lord would open up his armory/ arsenal of weapons of his indignation and, with them, gain victory in battle.

Now in present-day, our warfare is spiritual. Not carnal. Our weapons are however, STILL mighty though God to the pulling down of strong holds.

With you, The Lord will gain the victory.

VICTORY OBTAINED IN THE SPIRIT REALM:

The Lord is still our Battle Axe.

The weapons of our warfare are still Empowered, Anointed, Mighty, and Powerful (In the Lord) to break in pieces the nations (heathen) and destroy kingdoms.

WE WRESTLE NOT AGAINST FLESH AND BLOOD:

Wrestling: A contest between two in which each endeavor to throw the other, and which is decided when the victor is able to hold his opponent down with his hand upon his neck. The term is transferred to the struggle with the power of evil. Wrestling. Wrestle.

(Reference: Thayer/Strong's Definition)

We are not wrestling against mankind, but we are wrestling against the unseen realm, where we need the Power of the Lord in order to overcome. In order to gain Victory.

We wrestle against:

Principalities: The first person or thing in a series, the leader. Beginning, origin, the active cause, first place, principality, rule, (of angels or demons), first estate, magistrate, power, principle, rule.

Powers: Liberty of doing as one pleases, physical and mental power (the ability or strength with which one is endued, which he either possesses or exercises), ability, privilege, force, capacity, mastery, authority, right, jurisdiction, strength.

The Watchman's Position

Pose. Arrangement. Stance. Location.

See Below Reference Scriptures.

- 2 Corinthians 10:4
- Ephesians 6:12

Rulers of the Darkness of this world: lord of this world, prince of this age (the devil and his demons), world-ruler, an epithet of Satan. – ruler darkness, of darkened eyesight or blindness. Metaphorically of ignorance respecting divine things and human duties, and the accompanying ungodliness and immorality, together with their consequence misery or hell. Person in whom darkness becomes visible and holds away. Shadiness, obscurity, (literally or figuratively) darkness.

Spiritual Wickedness in high places: Supernatural, depravity, iniquity, malice, evil purposes and desires, plots, sins. Things that take place in the heavenlies, above the sky.

(Reference: Thayer/Strong's Definitions)

THE WHOLE ARMOR IS A WEAPON AS WELL AS A PROTECTION:

We are to cast off the works of darkness and put on the armor of Light.

The Lord has provided His children the armor of righteousness. The whole armor that we may STAND against the wiles of the devil. We must be strong in the Lord, and in the POWER of His Might.

We must STAND...

- Having our loins girt about with truth
- Having on the breastplate of righteousness
- Having our feet shod with the preparation of the gospel of peace
- **Above all** taking the shield of faith to quench the fiery darts of the wicked
- Taking the helmet of salvation
- Taking the sword of the spirit which is the word of God
- Praying always with prayer and supplication in the Spirit
- Watching with all perseverance and supplication for all saints

The Watchman's Position

Pose. Arrangement. Stance. Location.

See Below Reference Scriptures.

- Romans 13:12
- 2 Corinthians 6:7
- Ephesians 6: 13-18

INSTRUMENT OF PRAISE & WORSHIP

"He is thy praise, and he is thy God, that hath done for thee these great and terrible things, which thine eyes have seen."

(Deuteronomy 10:21) KJV

Your praise is the melody in your heart. God demands your praise. It is not optional. You praise the Lord because of HIS quality, deeds, and attributes. Praise the Lord, for blessed is the Lord God of Israel.

Praise and Worship are YOUR powerful Weapon:

With your body:

Present yourself a living sacrifice. Holy and acceptable unto the Lord. Which is... your reasonable service. We are to yield ourselves unto God as those who are alive from the dead. We are to yield our members as righteousness unto God.

Be careful to not yield your members as instruments of unrighteousness unto sin.

Call Upon the Lord:

Call upon the Lord for He is worthy to be praised. Call upon Him and be saved from your enemies.

Sing Praises Unto the Lord:

Sing praises unto His Name, and give thanks unto the Lord among the heathen.

Worship no other god:

Jehovah Elohim is a jealous God. His name is Jealous. Worship no other gods before Him.

71

The Watchman's Position

Pose. Arrangement. Stance. Location.

See Below Reference Scriptures.

- Romans 6:13
- 1 Chronicles 16:36
- 2 Samuel 22:4
- 2 Samuel 22:50
- Exodus 34:14

PRAYER BREAK/DELIVERANCE TIME:

(A prayer point can be given to individuals, or one designated person.)

Repent   Corporate Repentance (Everyone repent for your sins and the sins of your fathers.)

Converting: Turning from sin.

PRAYER POINTS:

Witchcraft/Jezebel: Works of the flesh/Projected diabolic energy aimed to shut the mouth of the Prophetic (Testimony of Jesus.) Rebellion/Disobedience

Ahab/Fear, Coward: Keeps you stagnant, stuck, and co-dependent, intimidated, dominated, and manipulated, flesh works

Mental Anguish: Rejection, Loneliness, Anxiety, flesh works

Emotional Turmoil: Depression, Oppression, flesh works

Spiritual Blockage: Discouragement, Pride, flesh works

Sexual Sins: (Whether it be as a single, or married person) Perversion, flesh works

Physical Neglect: Gluttony, Lazy, flesh works

Slothfulness/Sluggard: Despondent/Hopelessness, flesh works

(Be mindful, that being out of alignment with our Fathers uprightness, deems us out of compliance, and flesh works are INVOLVED. Be not deceived.)

Father,

God of my fathers, Abraham, Isaac, and Jacob, I give Your Name the glory that is due it. I present myself a living sacrifice unto You. Holy and acceptable which is my reasonable service. I come before You. And I worship You in the beauty of holiness.

In Jesus Name,

Amen

GROUP BREAK:

Allow space for Break-Out groups to form. In these groups, talk about what you have learned this far.

After the group Break is over, if time allows, give individuals the floor to discuss his/her observations, comments, and learnings.

<u>**Notes:**</u>

YOU WIN!

You Overcome!

GO FORTH MY FELLOW WATCHMAN!

SALVATION IS OF THE LORD GOD OF ISRAEL!

♥

SECTION 3

The Watchman's Challenges

THE WATCHMAN'S CHALLENGES

NOTES: At A Quick Glance:	**FEAR (TORMENTS, ADDICTIONS, PARALYSIS, 'STUCK')**
	• **Torments** • **Addictions** • **Paralysis 'Stuck'** *"For God has not given us a spirit of fear, but of power and of love and of a sound mind."* *(2 Timothy 1:7)* KJV
	Power: Strength, ability, abundance, miraculous power *LOVE:* Affection, benevolence, charity, brotherly love *Sound Mind:* Self-control, moderation, discipline (Reference: Thayer/Strong's Concordance)
	Fear is your enemy. You have **NOT** been given the spirit of fear, but of power, love, and sound mind.

TORMENTS

"There is no fear in love; but perfect love casts out fear, because fear involves torment. But he who fears has not been made perfect in love."

(1 John 4:18) NKJV

Fear: Dread, terror, that which strikes terror, alarm, afraid

Love: Brotherly love, affection, good will, benevolence, affection

Torment: Correction, punishment, penalty, penal affliction, punishment, torment

Made perfect: To carry through completely, to accomplish, finish, bring to an end, add what is yet wanting in order to render a thing full

(Reference: Thayer/Strong's Definition)

We are to love our brethren. We are to be 'perfect' even as our Father in heaven is perfect.

Saints are being made perfect for the work of the ministry and for edifying the body of Christ.

Being perfect implies full development. Growth into maturity in godliness. We are to handle ourselves and others in love and kindness and not sinful carnal impulses.

We are not children, we are not tossed to and fro by various doctrines, we are to; however speak the truth in love, and grow up in Christ. Christ is our head.

The Watchman's Challenges

Opposition. Confrontation With. Stand Against. Test Of.

See Below Reference Scriptures.

- Matthew 5:48
- Ephesians 4: 12
- Ephesians 4: 14

Notice conflicting pressure in your body, and remedy it.

Jezebel WILL attack you at times in your journey. You must know HOW TO stand against the **attack. You as a good solider must know HOW TO overcome by using your spiritual weapons of warfare that the LORD has provided.**

We must BE AWARE of the devices of the enemy.

One of these vices is... Discouragement (let's look at Elijah's story of discouragement.)

(1 Kings 19) NIV

"Elijah was afraid and ran for his life."

The demonic spirit of 'Rebellion/Witchcraft' that influenced Jezebel, wife of King Ahab, is still VERY ACTIVE today. (False prophets/teachers; male or female.) (Invisible forces affecting atmospheres). So be not deceived.

Jezebel (rebellion/witchcraft spirit) sends witchcraft mind assaults. Psychic attacks.

- Witchcraft is false teaching.
- Witchcraft is fear.

If the Jezebel spirit cannot get you to join her (as did the eunuchs) (and as she tried to entice Jehu); she will fight to shut down your influence. (As she did with Elijah).

Elijah had just executed great exploits for the LORD.

- Elijah prayed and caused it to not rain, and then prayed and caused it to rain.
- Elijah called down fire from heaven to demonstrate that the Lord Jehovah was the POWER behind the fire. The majestic SUPREMECY.
- Elijah destroyed the multitude of false prophets.

When Jezebel heard what Elijah had done, she sent witchcraft forces against him. Elijah was made to run for his life and buckle down under the force of psychic warfare.

The Watchman's Challenges

<u>Opposition. Confrontation With. Stand Against. Test Of.</u>

NOTES:

Elijah was supernaturally overwhelmed with fear and discouragement.

How did this happen?

Perhaps Elijah had experienced this before, or perhaps, it was Elijah's first experience with the diabolic gut wrenching fear. I believe that either way, Elijah did not know how to resist and contend with the supernatural influence that accompanied the words of Jezebel. Elijah's reaction was to run and not STAND against the assault. The psychic assault that sent him into retreat and hiding. **The witchcraft energy was able to get into Elijah's head.** Jehu on the other hand challenged the witchcraft energy.

- The 'craft' of the witch... induces energy.
- These energy forces are powerful demons working to psychologically paralyzed you.
- The energy force is piercing and heavy. Fearful.

From my experience, witchcraft attack will knock the breath out of you and disrupt your peace. Sending fear and the sensation that you are going to pass out. Supernaturally you will feel the demonic force/energy pressing your down. I would sometimes begin to be pressed down sideways. I would find myself fighting to remain upright in my position. (whether I am sitting or standing.)

During the time of attack, the supernatural environment around me would become suffocating and constricting. I would have to call upon the Lord for help and contend to keep the stealth force from causing me to pass out. (Even if it was a spiritual loss of consciousness that I had to recoup from.)

I will describe it as someone who's blood pressure drops and almost or does cause them to lose consciousness.

The Watchman's Challenges

Opposition. Confrontation With. Stand Against. Test Of.

Rest assured that whatever and whenever the attacks come... our Father has not left us. Nor have our Father forsaken us.

> The Lord gave me the revelation that...
>
> *Elijah story teaches us how the spirit attacks, and Jehu's story teaches us how to resist and defeat the spirit.*

The Jezebel/Witchcraft spirit (energy) is defeated by **THROWING IT DOWN.**

Jehu was raised up to defeat the house of Ahab and to destroy Jezebel.

The Jezebel spirit thrives on passive people that will not stand for the ways of truth and righteousness.

Be warned.

"He looked up at the window and called out, "Who is on my side? Who?" Two or three eunuchs looked down at him. "Throw her down!" Jehus said. So they threw her down, and some of her blood spattered the wall and the horses as they trampled her underfoot."

(2 Kings 9: 32-33) NIV

I didn't know what was happening for about a year. I thought I was having high anxiety and depression. But as I look back with understanding, the anxiety and depression were manifestations of the witchcraft psychic assault on my life during that intense season in my life.

I call it an intense season because at times I thought I was going to lose my mind. The season was real and the attack was real.

I endured (*with the WORD and Wonder Working Power of the Lord*) one of the hardest seasons in my life. (The Lord allowed it, and taught me through it, but it was scary and rigorous.)

Learning to fight this force was and has been hard. But I now fight with skill and confidence knowing that Greater is He in me... than he that is in the world.

As Watchmen, we are trained to be good soldiers. And to Overcome. WE have the VICTORY in Christ.

As a sidenote:

- I still encounter the psychic attacks here and there. I can perceive when witchcraft (the 'craft' of a witch) is present.
- Works of the flesh coming from someone else can sometimes be so strong to where I have to contend with the influence attempting to infiltrate/influence my mental reasoning and peace. THE UNCIRCUMSIZED GIANT RISING UP.
- The psychic attack can also be cast at you from afar. Witches, warlocks, generation curses, or besetting sin in your own life, can and will permit open door of entry. So be aware, and fight the good fight. No longer be afraid of the assault. When you perceive it... deal with it and DEFEAT it in Jesus Name.

The Watchman's Challenges

Opposition. Confrontation With. Stand Against. Test Of.

NOTES:

GROUP BREAK:

How Did/Do You my fellow Watchman experience Jezebel attack?

How Did/Do You contend?

(Feel free to share with the group.)

ADDICTIONS

Addiction: A strong and harmful need to regularly have something (such as a drug) or do something (such as gamble)

An unusually great interest in something or a need to have or do something

(Reference: Merriam-Webster Online)

Be not given to appetite. Do not succumb to gluttony.

Appetite: A natural desire to satisfy a bodily need, especially for food

A strong desire or liking for something

Appetite: The desire for food, stimulated by sight, smell or thought of food and accompanied by the flow of saliva in the mouth and gastric juices in the stomach

(Reference: Merriam-Webster/Medical Dictionary Online)

Gluttony: Habitual greed or excess in eating

(Reference: Online Dictionary)

Vocabulary.com reads... "Called one of the seven deadly sins, gluttony is characterized by a limitless appetite for food and drink and overindulgence to the point where one is no longer eating just to live, but rather living to eat."

The Watchman's Challenges

Opposition. Confrontation With. Stand Against. Test Of.

NOTES:

My advice is to...

- **Stop putting all that food in your mouth.**

Most people are overweight and sick because they OVEReat.

Eating is normal. OVEReating is SIN.

- **Practice self-control and fasting(s) unto the Lord.**

As a Watchman on the Wall, it is crucial that you allow the Lord to reign over your temple. (Your body.) We must be diligent to crucify our flesh and not be given to appetite.

- **Do not be given to Much wine DRUNKENESS/Excess.**

I believe that it is okay to have a social glass or two of wine. However, we are not to drink and drink in excess that causes us to lose control and become susceptible to temptation. We are to always be in our right mind to be able to watch and pray.

- **Outward appearance: VANITY**

Be aware of the TERROR of the MIRROR. Don't become 'in love' with the image in the mirror. Yes love yourself as well as others but steer away from being captivated and held prisoner to the pull of perpetually chasing fantasies and casting image for the mere applause and praises of society.

Look good... but don't lose your soul in the process. What profit is it to gain the world (approval), but lose your soul?

The Word of God is a roadmap for his Sons and Daughters. The Words contained in the Bible are for your good. Not to destroy you or be a hard slave driver. It is to instruct and guide you into safety and peace.

PARALYSIS 'STUCK'

WebMd.com reads that... *"Paralysis is when you can't move certain parts of your body after something goes wrong with their connection to your brain. It comes in many different forms and can be temporary or permanent or even come and go."*

Stuck: 1. Past simple or past particle of stick. 2. Unable to move, or set in a particular position

Stick: Adhere or cling to something

(Reference: dictionarycambridge.org/Online Dictionary)

A Watchman can sometimes find themselves 'stuck' in a particular position/place. Whether that position be others-induced, time & chance induced, God-induced, or Satan-induced.

We must choose to... handle (or deal with) the engagement/ trial/temptation speedily and not house it.

Get out of agreement with error quickly.

YOU/we, my fellow Watchman, have acquired the skill and ability to learn and move on. We are not to get slapped and trapped with a person, place, or thing,... choosing to adhere or cling to that particular unrighteous/toxic position.

> The role of a Watchman entails massive alone time, and intense strategic reasoning(s). A Watchman dwells inward.
>
> Inward reflection, inward contemplation, inward discernment and knowing.
>
> Careful to dwell and move in the Lord's safety. We engage, execute, and accomplish the Lord's WORK.

The Watchman's Challenges

Opposition. Confrontation With. Stand Against. Test Of.

"Therefore, my beloved brethren, be ye steadfast, unmovable, always abounding in the work of the Lord, forasmuch as ye know that your labour is not in vain in the Lord."

(1 Corinthians 15:58) KJV

- **Get rid of bitterness**
- **Get rid of unforgiveness**
- **Strengthen your bones:** *(There is no soundness in my flesh because of thine anger; neither is there any rest in my bones because of my sin.")* See Psalm 38:3 KJV
- **Heal from grief strickenness** *(For my life is spent with grief, and my years with sighing: my strength faileth because of mine iniquity, and my bones are consumed.")* See Psalm 31:10 KJV
- **Get rid of envy** *(A sound heart is the life of the flesh; but envy is as rottenness of the bone.)* See Proverbs 14:30 KJV

NOTES: At A Quick Glance:	**DESPONDENCY/DEPRESSION/EMOTIONAL ANGUISH** • **Cast cares upon the Lord** • **Double-minded (unstable)** • **Simple** *"His watchman are blind: they are all ignorant, they are all dumb dogs, they cannot bark; sleeping, lying down, loving to slumber."* *(Isaiah 56:10)* KJV ――――――――――― ――――――――――― **DESPONDENCY:** A state of low spirits caused by loss of hope or courage. **DEPRESSION:** Feelings of severe despondency and dejection. **EMOTIONAL:** Relating to a person's emotions. Arousing or characterized by intense feeling. **ANGUISH:** Severe mental or physical pain or suffering. Be extremely distressed about something. (Reference: Online Dictionary)

I would like to emphasize Isaiah 56: 10-12 again from the NIV version:

"Israel's watchmen are blind,

They all lack knowledge;

They are all mute dogs,

They cannot bark;

They lie around and dream,

They love to sleep.

They are dogs with mighty appetites;

They never have enough.

They are shepherds who lack understanding;

They all turn to their own way,

Each seeks his own gain.

"Come," each one cries, "let me get wine!

Let us drink our fill of beer!

And tomorrow will be like today, or ever far better."

CAST CARES UPON THE LORD

"Casting all your care upon him; for he careth for you."

(1 Peter 5:7) KJV

We are to cast our burden upon the Lord. The Lord WILL sustain us. Psalm 55 and 19 assures us that our Lord will not suffer the righteous to be moved.

Believe that God is... and that he is a rewarder of them that seek Him.

"There is no man that hath power over the spirit to retain the spirit, neither hath he power in the day of death: and there is no discharge in that war: neither shall wickedness deliver those that are given to it."

(Ecclesiastes 8:8) KJV

I would like to expound more on the importance of your emotional and mental health. It is very important to have the confidence of Christ, have single vision, and to trust in the Lord with all your heart.

In the hedge of the Lord's protection is where YOUR peace is. The hedge of the Lord's protection is where YOUR soundness of mind is.

The Lord has promised to keep us in His perfect peace. If we keep our mind stayed on Him. We are to trust in the Lord Jehovah forever. HE IS EVERLASTING STRENGTH.

The Watchman's Challenges

Opposition. Confrontation With. Stand Against. Test Of.

See Below Referenced Scriptures.

- Isaiah 26: 3-4

DOUBLE-MINDED (UNSTABLE)

"A double-minded man is unstable in all his ways."

(James 1:8) KJV

A wavering man is like a wave of the sea driven with the wind and tossed to and fro. That man should not think that he will receive anything of the Lord.

Double-mindedness is a 'sickness' of the heart. A heart condition that affects the inner man.

Double-mindedness cannot be remedied with and by nothing but the redeeming Blood of Jesus. The heart will have to be cleansed/transformed, healed, and acclimated to spiritual structure... <u>IN</u> Christ.

The mind will need to be renewed.

When a person is double-minded, <u>instability</u> is the sign. A person will be unstable.

Unstable: Likely to change or fail; not firmly established, likely to give way, not stable; prone to psychiatric problems or sudden changes of mood.

<u>Synonyms:</u>   Rocky, unsafe, wobbly, unbalanced, insecure, movable, unpredictable, uncertain, deranged, demented, crazed, distracted, troubled, insane, mad.

When double-minded, the mind is wrestling with two opposing views. A double-mind is the same as having a double-heart.

"They speak vanity every one with his neighbor: with flattering lips and with a double heart do they speak."

(Psalm 12:2) KJV

<u>**Opposition. Confrontation With. Stand Against. Test Of.**</u>

See Below Referenced Scriptures.

- James 1: 6-7

Being firm and solid in your mind/reasoning/decisions is to not have a double-heart. Is to not have a double-mind.

A double-minded man lives by a double-standard. Two-faced. And is deceitful. A double-minded man is not faithful and cannot be trusted. When you perceive a double-mind, trust that along with the person is half-hearted allegiance. (Even if it happens to be the man/woman in the mirror.)

DO NOT PUT YOUR CONFIDENCE IN A DOUBLE-MINDED PERSON.

"Confidence in an unfaithful man in time of trouble is like a broken tooth, and a foot out of joint."

(Proverbs 25:19) KJV

My fellow Watchman, the remedy to double-mindedness is to resolve today to believe and trust in the Lord with all your heart, with all your soul, and with all your might. We are to be single-minded and single-hearted. The Lord will not allow your foot to be moved. In the Lord's care we can rest in blessed assurance that we are safe. We can STAND FIRM.

We must believe in our Lord and what He has and is doing in us and in the world, and proceed forward in the confidence of Christ.

We must allow the Lord to be our HOPE for tomorrow and our STRENGTH for today.

You cannot serve two masters.

How long halt ye between two opinions?

The Watchman's Challenges

Opposition. Confrontation With. Stand Against. Test Of.

See Below Referenced Scriptures.

- 1 Chronicles 12:33
- Acts 2:46
- Ephesians 6:5
- Colossians 3:22
- Psalm 121:3
- Matthew 6:24
- Mark 12:30
- 1 Kings 18:21

"Hear, O Israel: The LORD our God is one LORD:
And thou shalt love the LORD thy God with all thine heart, and with all thy soul, and with all thy might."

(Deuteronomy 6: 4-5) KJV

SIMPLE

The law of the Lord is perfect, converting the soul: the testimony of the Lord is sure, making wise the simple.

(Psalm 19:7) KJV

Simple: Simplicity, naivete, foolish, open-minded, silly (that is, seducible).

Reference: BDB/Strong's Definition)

How long you simple ones, will you love simplicity?

One must allow the entrance of the Lord's Words to give light and understanding.

> ***"For the turning away of the simple shall slay them, and the prosperity of fools shall destroy them."***

(Proverbs 1:32) KJV

It's time to let the simple mindedness go and understand wisdom.

- The simple minded, inherits folly
- The hearts of the simple are easily deceived

Be wise unto that which is good, and simple concerning evil.

THE WATCHMAN'S CHALLENGES: *Continued*

NOTES: At A Quick Glance:	DISTRACTION TO KEEP YOU UN-ENGAGED IN BATTLE • **Carnal** • **Lovers of self** • **Lovers of the world** *"Yea, they are greedy dogs which can never have enough, and they are shepherds that cannot understand: they all look to their own way, every one for his gain, from his quarter."* *(Isaiah 56:11)* KJV --- **Distraction:** A thing that prevents someone from giving full attention to something else. **Engaged**: Fully occupied or having your full attention. **Battle:** To engage in combat between individuals or armed forces: to engage in battle. (Reference: Online Dictionary)

CARNAL

"For to be carnally minded is death; but to be spiritually minded is life and peace."

(Romans 8:6) KJV

Carnal: Fleshly, carnal, having the nature of flesh;, i.e. under the control of the animal appetites, governed by mere human nature not by the Spirit of God, bodily, temporal, unregenerate, carnal, fleshly.

Carnally: The sensuous nature of man, "the animal nature" the flesh, human nature (with its frailties (physically or morally) and passions)

(Reference: Thayer/Strong's Definition)

To be carnally minded is to be in opposition to the ways of the Lord. Being carnally minded makes one hostile, and positions one in a <u>posture</u> of hatred to the ways of the Lord.

The laws of the Lord are spiritual, so one must come out of carnality which postures one still sold under sin. Carnality keeps one captive to envying, strife, and divisions. Keeping one walking as men.

Always be mindful that the weapons of our warfare are NOT carnal. But are MIGHTY through God to the pulling down of strongholds.

There is no way that one can please the Lord in a stance of carnality. We approach the Lord in spirit and in truth. One's carnal nature will never enter in.

The Watchman's Challenges

<u>**Opposition. Confrontation With. Stand Against. Test Of.**</u>

See Below Referenced Scriptures.

- Romans 8:7
- Romans 7:14
- 1 Corinthians 3:3
- 2 Corinthians 10:4

LOVERS OF SELF

For men shall be lovers of their own selves, covetous, boasters, proud, blasphemers, disobedient to parents, unthankful, unholy.

(2 Timothy 3:2) KJV

Lovers of their own selves: *Fond of self, that is, selfish Loving one's self. Too intent on one's interest. Selfish.*

Covetous: Loving money.

Boasters: Braggert. Empty pretender. Boaster.

Proud: Showing one's self above others. Overweening estimate of one's means or merits, despising others or even treating them with contempt, haughty.

Blasphemer: Speaking evil, slanderous, reproachful, railing, abusive

Disobedient: Unpersuadable. Disobedient

Unthankful: Ungracious. Unpleasing. Unthankful. Thankless

Unholy: Wicked

Traitors, heady, high-minded, lovers of pleasures more than lovers of God. (2 Timothy 3:4) KJV

Traitors: Betrayer. (in the sense of giving forward into another's [the enemy's] hands)

Heady: Reckless

High-minded: To blind with pride or conceit, to render foolish or stupid. To make proud, puff up with pride.

Lovers of Pleasures: Loving pleasure. Fond of pleasure, that is, voluptuous. Lover of pleasure.

The Watchman's Challenges

<u>**Opposition. Confrontation With. Stand Against. Test Of.**</u>

NOTES:

More than…

Lovers of God: Loving God. Fond of God, Lover of God.

(Reference: Strong's/Thayer Definition)

BODILY EXERCISE

"For bodily exercise profiteth little: but godliness is profitable unto all things, having promise of the life that now is, and of that which is to come." (1 Timothy 4:8) KJV

Reference and respect toward God is profitable over all things. Bodily exercise is good, but we must keep a healthy balance and remember that godliness is the GOAL. Our character is what will speak for us. Our bodies will perish, but our spirit is eternal.

The Watchman's Challenges

Opposition. Confrontation With. Stand Against. Test Of.

"Wherefore God also gave them up to uncleanness through the lusts of their own hearts, to dishonor their own bodies between themselves."

(Romans 1:24) KJV

"Ye ask, and receive not, because ye ask amiss, that ye may consume it upon your lusts."

(James 4:3) KJV

LOVERS OF THE WORLD

"Teaching us that, denying ungodliness and worldly lusts, we should live soberly, righteously and godly, in this present world."

(Titus 2:12) KJV

Denying: Not accept. Reject, refuse something offered

Ungodliness: Wickedness

Worldly: Of or belonging to the world. Worldly, i.e. having the character of this present corrupt age

Lusts: Desire, craving, longing, desire for what is forbidden

Soberly: With sound mind, temperately, discreetly

Righteously: Just. Agreeable to right. Uprightly. Agreeable to the law of rectitude

Godly: Piously. Godly

Present: At this time, the present. Now

World: The worlds. Universe. Period of time. Age

"So I gave them up unto their own hearts' lust: and they walked in their own counsels." (Psalm 81:12) KJV

Lust: *Stubbornness, hardness, firmness.*
In the sense of twisted, that is, firm; obstinacy; Imagination.

Counsel: *Counsel, plan, principal, device.*
Purpose

(Reference: Strong's/BDB Definition)

The Watchman's Challenges

<u>**Opposition. Confrontation With. Stand Against. Test Of.**</u>

NOTES:

The Lord will give a person up and allow them to be taken by their own lusts. We must be careful to make no provision for the flesh to fulfil its lusts. We must instead walk in the Spirit that we do not fulfil the lust of the flesh.

"For all that is in the world, the lust of the flesh, and the lust of the eyes, and the pride of life, is not of the Father, but is of the world." (1 John 2:16) KJV

Lust: Desire, craving, longing, desire for what is forbidden, lust.

Of the flesh: The flesh denotes mere human nature, the earthly nature of man apart from divine influence, and therefore prone to sin and opposed to God.

Of the eyes: The eye. Metaphorically the eyes of the mind, the faculty of knowing; figuratively envy (from the jealous side glance): Sight.

Pride of Life: Empty braggart talk. Self-confidence, boasting, pride.

                    An insolent and empty assurance, which trusts in its own power and resources and shamefully despises and violates divine laws and human rights. Trusts in the stability of earthly things.

Those who live in error will use great swelling words of vanity to try and allure us through the lusts of the flesh. Watchmen, we must remain clear that we may escape.

Remember there will be mockers in the last time who walk after their own lusts.

The Watchman's Challenges

Opposition. Confrontation With. Stand Against. Test Of.

Every man is tempted when he is drawn away of his own lust and enticed. When lust is conceived, it brings forth sin. And remember... when sin is finished... it brings forth death.

RECAP/PRAYER/ACTIVATION/RESORATION

RECAP:

Many Watchmen need to:

- Repent.

To be sorry, regret

- Convert

To return, turn back, restore, be brought back

(Reference: BDB/Strong's Definition)

- Get back on the Wall and go forward in the name of the LORD.

PRAYER: (To seal what has been taught.)

ACTIVATION/RESORATION: (Prophesy and Declare what the Lord has decreed.)

"Therefore my beloved brethren, be ye steadfast, unmovable, always abounding in the work of the Lord, forasmuch as ye know, that your labor is not in vain in the Lord."

(1 Corinthians 15:58) KJV

Thank You for Supporting the Work that I have been given to do in the earth.

Printed in the United States
by Baker & Taylor Publisher Services